D0248950

Quick Children's Sermons: Will My Dog Be in Heaven?

Group

Loveland, Colorado

Quick Children's Sermons:
Will My Dog Be in Heaven?

Copyright © 1997 Group Publishing, Inc. / 0000 0001 0362 4853

All rights reserved. No part of this book may be reproduced in any manner whatsoever without prior written permission from the publisher, except where noted in the text and in the case of brief quotations embodied in critical articles and reviews. For information, visit group.com/permissions.

Visit our website: **group.com**

CREDITS
Contributing Authors: Robin Christy, Mary Davis, Ken Kellner, Jr., Cynthia A. Kenney, Mary J. Kurth, Lori Haynes Niles, Linda Stephan, and Bonnie Temple
Book Acquisitions Editor: Susan L. Lingo
Editors: Mary Van Aalsburg and Jody Brolsma
Managing Editor: Paul Woods
Chief Creative Officer: Joani Schultz
Copy Editor: Julie Meiklejohn
Art Director and Designer: Jean Bruns
Cover Art Director: Helen H. Lannis
Computer Graphic Artist: Kari K. Monson
Cover Designer: Diana Walters
Cover Illustrator: Stacey Lamb
Production Manager: Ann Marie Gordon

Unless otherwise noted, Scriptures quoted from The Youth Bible, New Century Version, copyright © 1991 by Word Publishing, Dallas, Texas 75039. Used by permission.

Library of Congress Cataloging-in-Publication Data
Quick children's sermons : will my dog be in heaven?
      p.   cm.
   Includes indexes.
   ISBN 978-1-55945-612-8
   1. Children's sermons. I. Group Publishing.
BV4315.Q53 1997
252'.53--dc21   96-48437
                                             CIP

30 29   20 19

Printed in the United States of America.

Contents

Questions Kids Ask About the Bible

Questions Kids Ask About Life

Introduction

Does God take naps?
Was Jesus rich?
Will God love me no matter what?

Kids ask some of the silliest questions! But are they really so silly? Haven't we all wondered at one time or another if Jesus was there with us in some sticky situation? The quick, simple, down-to-earth answers kids want and need will also touch the hearts of adults who "listen in."

Quick Children's Sermons: Will My Dog Be in Heaven? is filled with fun, active, kid-centered answers to some of those off-the-wall questions children throw at us every day. Each sermon is based on a biblical response to a question and geared to keep kids' attention while encouraging their participation and accepting their wiggles. In addition, the "Simple Supplies" section found in each sermon requires little preparation.

You won't want to limit the use of these active-learning messages to Sunday mornings. They're great for church-family gatherings, Sunday school teachers' meetings, children's church or Sunday school openers, or even quick staff devotionals. Anyone who loves children will enjoy sharing these sermons with kids of all ages.

Jesus said, "Let the little children come to me" (Luke 18:16b). Gather the children, and have some fun on Sunday morning or any time as you share God's truth by answering questions that come straight from the heart of the child in each of us.

Questions
Kids Ask
About

God

Theme:
We are all equally important to God.

What Color Shoes Does God Like?

Bible Reference:
James 2:1-4

Simple Supplies:
A Bible; many pairs of shoes in a variety of styles (make sure that you have at least one pair of nice, fancy shoes and at least one pair of old, dirty shoes); a watch or stopwatch; and foot-shaped stickers

Set out a pile of many different pairs of shoes. Let's play a game with these shoes. We'll see how fast you can find pairs of shoes and line them up neatly. *Show the children where to line up the shoes so everyone can see them, and have the children line up single-file.* When I say "Go," the first two people in line will run to the pile of shoes. Each person will find a pair of shoes in the pile and then place the shoes neatly on the line. When the first two people are finished, they'll walk back to the starting line, and the next two people will go. We'll continue this way until all the shoes are lined up. I'll time you. *If you have more children than pairs of shoes, ask for as many volunteers as you have pairs of shoes.*

Great job! It only took __ minutes. *Fill in the blank with the number of minutes it took the kids to finish the task.* Now that I can see all these shoes so clearly, I'm going to pick out the pair of shoes I want to wear when I go to heaven.

Pick up a fancy pair of shoes. Raise your hand if you think I could get into heaven wearing this fancy pair of shoes. Why? *Allow a few children to share their thoughts. Hold up an old, dirty pair of shoes.* Scratch your nose if you think I could get into heaven wearing this old, dirty pair of shoes. Why? *Allow a few children to share their thoughts.* Tap your head if you think God doesn't look at your shoes.

God talks about this very thing in the book of James. Turn to James 2:1-4 in your Bible. Listen to this: "My dear brothers and sisters . . . never think some people are more important than others. Suppose someone comes into your church meeting wearing nice clothes and a gold ring. At the same time a poor person comes in wearing old, dirty clothes. You show special attention to the one wearing nice clothes and say, 'Please, sit here in this good seat.' But you say to the poor person, 'Stand over there,' or, 'Sit on the floor by my feet.' What are you doing? You are making some people more important than others, and with evil thoughts you are deciding that one person is better."

So let's imagine that I'm standing at heaven's gates with this dirty old pair of shoes on. According to the verses I just read, how would God respond to my shoes? *Let the children respond.* That's right. These dirty old shoes wouldn't matter to God. God loves and accepts me regardless of how I look or how I'm dressed. He doesn't have a favorite color of shoes.

Now let's say a new person comes to your school or church. How do you decide if they are nice or if you want to be friends with them? *Let a few children share.* How do you think God would treat a new person? *Allow children to share their thoughts.*

Let's close in prayer by asking God to help us love and accept all people regardless of how they dress or look.

❤ **Dear God, thank you for loving us just for who we are. Help us not to judge others based on their appearances. Teach us to love like you love and to look at others as you look at others. Teach us to be kind and accepting to all different kinds of people. We want to obey your Word. Amen.** ❤

I have a foot-shaped sticker that I want to give to you. *Distribute the foot-shaped stickers.* Take the sticker home as a reminder that God doesn't judge us by how we look, so we need to not judge others by how they look. We need to accept and love others even though they appear to be different from us.

Theme:
God is always awake, watching and guarding us.

Does God Take Naps?

Bible Reference:
Psalm 121:3-4 and John 10

Simple Supplies:
A Bible, a beloved stuffed animal, and one paper cutout of an eye for each child (p. 11)

Today I have brought a special buddy to show you. This is my precious teddy bear *(or another beloved stuffed animal)* that I've had for a very long time. Teddy has been through many difficult and happy times with me. I want to pass Teddy around and let you hold him gently. Teddy is getting old, so I need to take good care of him. What kind of harm could come upon my teddy bear? How do you think I would feel if I let harm come upon him? *Let the children respond.*

Open your Bible to John 10. In John 10, Jesus talks about how we are his precious sheep and he is our Good Shepherd. He takes care of us by leading us to food and water. He knows us by name, and we know his gentle, loving voice. He leads us, and we follow him. He protects us from robbers and wolves. Even at night when we are sleeping and the most vulnerable to attack, Jesus never sleeps. He stays awake all the time to watch over us. *Open your Bible to Psalm 121:3-4.* Psalm 121:3-4 says: "He will not let you be defeated. He who guards you never sleeps. He who guards Israel never rests or sleeps." What a wonderful promise of protection.

Now I want you to imagine something with me. It's a dark and stormy night. Thunder is crashing. Make thunder noises with me by stomping your feet. Lightning is streaking across the sky. Sheets of rain are dousing the windows. Snap your fingers to make rain. Now close your eyes, and try to imagine going to sleep with the storm going on. How do you feel on nights like these? How does it make you feel to remember that God never sleeps but is watching over you? *Let the children respond.*

Raise your hand if you have ever felt alone. Maybe you were lost in a store or a mall or you were feeling left out by your friends. How do you feel, knowing that God is guarding you all the time? *Let the children respond.*

Can you tell me about a time you felt afraid? *Let the children respond.* Let's say our verse together: *Have the children echo you after each sentence.* "He will not let you be defeated. He who guards you never sleeps. He who guards Israel never rests or sleeps."

Let's close in prayer by telling God how we feel about his protection.

💜 **Dear God, thank you for guarding us always. We sure are grateful that you will not let us be defeated and that you preserve our lives. Thank you for keeping us safe. Amen.** 💜

Here is a paper eye. It is always open, watching and guarding and never sleeping. When you look at this eye, remember that God is always awake, guarding your life. *Distribute paper eyes to the children.*

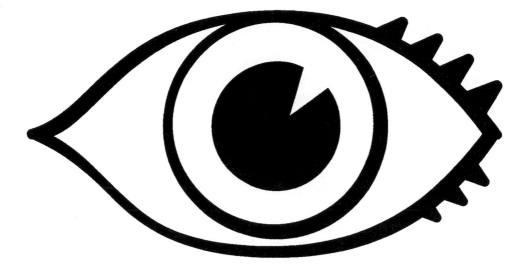

Permission to photocopy this pattern from *Quick Children's Sermons: Will My Dog Be in Heaven?* granted for local church use. Copyright © Group Publishing, Inc., P.O. Box 481, Loveland, CO 80539.

Theme:
God is always by my side.

Bible Reference:
Psalm 139:7-10

Simple Supplies:
A Bible and a deflated beach ball

Where Does God Go For His Summer Vacation?

Have you ever felt like you wanted to take a break from school, your family, or your friends? What would you do to get away? Where would you go? As I blow up this beach ball, be thinking about your responses to these questions. *Inflate the ball.* Now I'm going to pass the ball around. When the ball comes to you, tell us where you would go to get away for a while. *Let several or all of the children have a turn.*

Even when we get away, God is still with us. I'm glad that he is.

Do you think that God would ever like to take a break from us? *Allow a few children to respond.* Let's discover what King David knew about God's presence with us. *Open your Bible to Psalm 139:7-10.* In Psalm 139:7-10, David describes how God is everywhere. Let's do some motions as I read this psalm. Stand up and follow me.

Where can I go to get away from your Spirit? Where can I run from you? *Run in place.* If I go up to the heavens *(raise hands up high),* you are there. If I lie down in the grave *(lie down),* you are there.

If I rise with the sun in the east and settle in the west beyond the sea *(stretch arms out to the sides),* even there you would guide me. With your right hand you would hold me. *Clasp hands together.*

God doesn't just "camp out" in one place or another. How does it make you feel to know that God is everywhere, all the time? *Let the children share.*

I feel comforted because I know that God is always present. I remind myself that God is by my side, he's my friend and companion, and he loves me without conditions. He never takes a vacation or a day off! He is always there for me.

Let's put our right hands in the middle of a group circle *(like a team huddle),* and thank God for holding us with his right hand.

💗 **Dear God, thank you for always being with us and for never taking a day off. We can count on you to be there for us, and we praise you. Amen.** 💗

Let's close our prayer by saying "Yeah, God!" *Say "Yeah, God!" as a sports team would say "Go, Team!" at the end of a team huddle.*

Theme:
*God provides all
we need.*

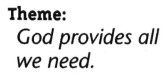
When Does God Eat Dinner?

Bible Reference:
Philippians 4:19

Simple Supplies:
A Bible, a lunch box, a whole apple, and apple slices

What are some things we need to stay alive? *Let children respond.* What are some of your favorite foods? Do you think God has a favorite food? What would he like for breakfast? *Hold up a lunch box.* What might God take in his lunch box? What do you think he eats for dinner? *Let children respond to each question.* I wonder if God really does eat dinner?

Hold up the apple, and take a bite of it. This juicy apple is one of the things God has provided. It's sweet and crunchy—a wonderful gift from God. We can eat it as it is, or we can use it to make other foods. What else can we make with apples? *Let children respond. Their answers may include such things as applesauce, pie, jelly, and salad.*

Do you think God likes to eat apples? We don't really know, do we? God doesn't need food, water, or shelter because he is Spirit. But God knows that we need things like food, shelter, water, and love. And he has made us a promise. *Open your Bible to Philippians 4:19.* Philippians 4:19 says, "My God will use his wonderful riches in Christ Jesus to give you everything you need."

Next time you eat an apple, I hope it will remind you to thank God for all he's given you. Let's close in prayer.

💜 **Dear God, we thank you today for all the wonderful gifts you've given us, such as food, shelter, our families, and each other. Most of all, we thank you for you. Help us to remember to thank you each day for the many blessings you've given us. In Jesus' name, amen.** 💜

Distribute the apple slices. Take an apple slice before you leave, and remember as you eat it that God provides all we need.

Theme:

God is our Creator who made everything good.

How Did God Make the World in Seven Days?

Bible Reference:

Genesis 1:1

Simple Supplies:

A Bible, a walnut-sized piece of modeling clay for each child, a watch or stopwatch, and a plastic sandwich bag for each child

W hat does a creator do? *Allow the children to respond.* How many of you think of yourselves as creators? I have a small piece of modeling clay for each of you. I'd like you to create something using this modeling clay. But you only have a minute to do it! Are you ready? *Distribute the pieces of modeling clay, and allow the children one minute to make something with their pieces of clay. After one minute, ask the children to hold up their creations for everyone to see.*

Look at all the different things you were able to come up with in just one minute! That was really good! How does it feel to create something good? *Let kids respond.*

The first story in the Bible tells us God created the world in seven days. He made something out of nothing, and it was all very good. How do you think he did that? *Let kids offer suggestions.*

Time means different things to different people. For example, while the congregation waited for you to create something with your modeling clay, they probably thought a minute was a long time. But when you were trying to create something good in just one minute, it probably felt like a very short time to you.

Open your Bible to Genesis 1:1. Genesis 1:1 reads, "In the beginning God created the sky and the earth." God isn't limited in what he can do like humans are. He can create whatever he wants as quickly as he wants.

The most important thing to remember is that God is our Creator. God made things beautiful and perfect, and he placed us in the world to enjoy it and take care of it!

Let's close with a prayer. During the prayer, I'd like you to name a part of God's creation you enjoy, and we'll thank him for it together. Ready?

♥ **Dear God, thank you for being our Creator. You made all things good! We'd especially like to thank you for:** *Let kids call out* *things they are thankful for and then all together shout* **Amen!** ♥

I have a plastic sandwich bag for each of you to use to store your modeling clay. *Give each child a plastic sandwich bag.* Each time you create something new with your clay, remember that God is our Creator!

GO THE EXTRA MILE! Prepare your own "stove top" modeling clay to keep down the expense. In a medium pot, mix 1 cup white flour, ¼ cup salt, and 2 tablespoons cream of tartar. Add 1 cup water, 2 teaspoons food coloring, and 1 tablespoon oil. Cook over medium heat, stirring frequently, for three to five minutes. It will look like a messy glob. When it forms a ball in the center of your pan, turn it out on a floured surface and knead it until smooth. Store it in an airtight bag or container. It's easy to make, and it's edible, though not very tasty.

Theme:

We're created to praise God!

Bible Reference:

Revelation 1:8

How Old Is God?

Simple Supplies:

A Bible, a birthday cake or one cupcake for each child, napkins, and at least one birthday candle for each child. If you choose to bring a birthday cake, be sure you have a knife to cut it.

Do you like birthday parties? Why do we have birthday parties? *Let the children respond.* Birthday parties are to celebrate the birth of someone special. We're thankful that person was born and is part of our lives!

What's your favorite thing to do at a birthday party? *Wait for responses.* Sometimes we play games, eat, and sing. I have an idea. How about if we have a birthday party for God?

I'd like to celebrate all the wonderful things God has done for us and to sing his praises! Does anyone like birthday cake? *Look around as if you're waiting for one of the kids to bring out a cake.* Well, I just happen to have one for our celebration! *Bring out your cake or cupcakes.* And I have lots of birthday candles. *Give a candle to each child.* How many candles should we put on the cake? Does anyone know how old God is? *Look perplexed. Ask the kids to count out candles and decide how many to use on the cake.* Do you think we have enough candles here to put on God's birthday cake? *Get kids' reaction.*

We read in the Bible about Creation, but we're not told about the beginning of God. *Open your Bible to Revelation 1:8.* Revelation 1:8 says: "The Lord God says, 'I am the Alpha and the Omega. I am the One who is and was and is coming. I am the Almighty.' " God has always been. He was never born, so he doesn't have birthdays. God's age doesn't really matter. God loves us, takes care of us, and sent his son Jesus to live and die for us!

Let's celebrate today by singing a praise prayer to the tune of "Happy Birthday." It goes like this:

♥ **We praise you today! We praise you today! We praise you, dear God; We praise you always!** ♥

Let the children sing the song through with you the second time, and then invite the congregation to join in the third time.

Take your candle home today. On your next birthday, put it on your cake as a special invitation to God to be with you on your special day!

Pass out cupcakes or pieces of cake and napkins.

Theme:
God hears each one of us!

Bible Reference:
1 John 5:14

Simple Supplies:
A Bible, an ear of corn in its husk (or a picture if corn is not available); a variety of items made with corn, such as cornflakes, corn dogs, popcorn, popcorn cakes, corn tortillas, and caramel corn; and small bags of popcorn for a treat and a fun reminder of this message

How Can God Listen to Everyone at the Same Time?

I love corn! *Hold up the ear of corn for the children to see.* Fresh-picked corn, cooked just right, dripping with butter—yum! Lots of great things to eat are made with corn. What's your favorite? *Let kids respond, and hold up items as you or the children think of them.*

Corn grows on "ears," but they don't look much like our ears. How do our ears help us? *Let kids respond.* Think about all the things that you heard this morning—a call to get up, prayers at breakfast, talking with family members, and songs here at church. I'll count to three, and I'd like everyone to shout out something you heard this morning. All together now—ready? One, two, three! *When everyone shouts, you probably won't really* **hear** *anyone. Turn to several individual children, and ask each this question:* "(Child's name), what did (another child's name) say?" *Allow responses to all questions.* Why is this so hard?

We can't hear everyone at once, but God can. God has some pretty powerful ears! God can listen to all of us at the same time. *Open your Bible to 1 John 5:14.* 1 John 5:14 says, "And this is the boldness we have in God's presence: that if we ask God for anything that agrees with what he wants, he hears us." We can't explain how God hears so much at once, but we know it's true because the Bible tells us it is.

Ears of corn are great for eating, and our ears work well to hear things around us, but God's ears allow him to listen to everyone at the same time.

♥ For our closing prayer, I'll count to three, and all of you will say, **"Thank you, God, for hearing our prayers."** OK—one, two, three! *Let kids shout the prayer.* And we all say together: **Amen!** ♥

As a reminder of God's ever-listening ears, I'm giving each of you a small bag of popcorn. *Give each child a bag of popcorn.* Each time you eat corn, stop and thank God for the blessing of good things to eat and for the special promise that his ears are always ready to listen to us when we talk to him.

Theme:
God answers our prayers.

Bible Reference:
Psalm 5:3b and Matthew 6:8b

Does God Answer My Prayers?

Simple Supplies:
A Bible, two phones (toy or real), and a few catalogs

Have any of you ever ordered anything from a catalog? *Hold up a catalog.* It's a good way to get things you need. How do you reach the catalog company to place your order? *After kids answer, hold up a phone.* Can you see the person at the other end? After you place your order, how long do you have to wait? *Let children respond to all questions.*

Give catalogs to two or more volunteers, and ask them to choose things they want or need. Have each volunteer use one phone and pretend to call the catalog company. You will be the "catalog company operator" on the other phone. Take children's orders, but occasionally respond by saying, "What you really need is *(name something from their catalog, such as long underwear),* because *(give a reason, such as "you will be taking a trip to Alaska this winter.")*

What was strange about the operator? How did you feel when the operator told you what you needed? Would you like it if someone knew what you really needed and got it ready for you before you even asked? *Allow kids to respond to all questions.* Well, God does this. *Open your Bible to Matthew 6:8.* Matthew writes that when you pray, God not only hears you, but he has been waiting for you to call! Matthew 6:8b tells us, "Your Father knows the things you need before you ask him."

Sometimes when you order from a catalog, what you get is a little different than what you expected. Prayer can be like that. God's answers can be "yes," "no," or "wait." The answer God gives to your prayer might be different than the answer you imagined. Answers to prayer can take time, too. *Open your Bible to Psalm 5:3b.* Psalm 5:3b says, "Every morning, I tell you what I need, and I wait for your answer."

God hears our prayers, and he knows what we need and when we need it. Let's pray. We know God will be listening!

♥ *Let volunteers take turns using the phone to say to God, "God, thank you for answering our prayers!" Close with:* **Dear God, we're excited that you are thinking about us, want the best for us, and know what we need. We look forward to your answers to our prayers. Help us to be patient and to listen to you. In Jesus' name, amen.** ♥

Theme:
God is invisible, yet we know he exists.

Is God Invisible?

Bible Reference:
Romans 1:20a

Simple Supplies:
A Bible; a blow-dryer with a cool setting; and a pingpong ball, balloon, or small beach ball. For extra fun, decorate the ball to look like the Earth.

What are some things you can't see but you know are there? *Let children respond.* Some powerful, invisible things I know of are radio waves, germs, and sound. A strong gust of wind is invisible, but it can knock a big truck on its side.

Turn the blow-dryer on cool, and point it straight up. Put the pingpong ball (or balloon or beach ball) in the stream of air until it is held up by the air. Have kids try these three things:

1. Push the ball gently with one finger from the side.

2. Tilt the blow-dryer at a 45° angle.

3. Place a hand in the way of the airstream.

Can you see air? How do we know the air is there? How powerful is air? Invisible air can lift up a huge plane. When you put your hand in the airstream, can you feel the air? *Allow kids to respond to all questions.*

Just as the invisible airstream held up this pingpong ball and can hold up a big airplane, our invisible God created the world around us. We can't see the air holding up the ball, but we know it's there. We can't see God, but we know he's there because he takes care of us.

The Bible says that God is invisible. How do we know that God is there even though we can't see him? *Let children respond. Open your Bible to Romans 1:20a.* Romans 1:20a tells us, "There are things about him that people cannot see—his eternal power and all the things that make him God. But since the beginning of the world those things have been easy to understand by what God has made."

Even though God is invisible, we know he exists because of the things he has made—the sun, the moon, the stars, and the animals. We know he is there because his power shines down on us as the warmth of the sun and swirls around us as the wind. We know God is here with us, even though we can't see him.

Let's close in prayer, thanking God for always being with us.

❤ **Dear God, we are amazed at the things you have created.**

We can see, hear, and touch the world around us and understand what a wonderful Creator you are. Thank you for the comfort of knowing that you are with us all the time. In Jesus' name, amen. ❤️

Pretend to pass out a "handful of air" to each person. Tell them to keep the air cupped in their hands or it will escape. Tell them to be careful with their air, as it can knock over buildings, lift airplanes, and break concrete.

Theme:
God created all things good.

Bible Reference:
Psalm 8:3

Simple Supplies:
A Bible, a piece of poster board for every three or four kids, lots of colorful star stickers, and markers

How Did God Get All the Stars in the Right Places?

Do you ever sit outside at night and look up into the starry sky? What shapes have you seen? *Allow children to respond.* Groups of stars are called constellations. Some of the most famous constellations are Orion, the Big Dipper, and the Little Dipper. Have you ever seen these? Can you name any other constellations? *Allow children to respond.*

Let's make our own constellations and name each of the stars in them.

Have kids form groups of three or four. Hand each child four or five star stickers, and give one piece of poster board and several markers to each group. Tell groups they have about two minutes to stick their stars on the poster board, name each star, and name their constellations. Help kids write on the poster board.

What was it like to name all the stars? You struggled to put up *(rough number of stars)* stars and name them. How many stars do you think God put up in the sky? *Let kids respond.* God put more than a billion billion stars in the sky. David wrote in the Psalms that God determined the number of stars and called them each by name. How do you think he came up with so many names?

Open your Bible to Psalm 8:3. The Bible says in Psalm 8:3, "I look at your heavens, which you made with your fingers. I see the moon and stars, which you created." God put a billion billion stars up by himself! Some stars are one thousand times larger than the sun. God named every one.

God is truly awesome. He created the stars, gave them names, and put them in the right places. And we know they're in the right places because God doesn't make mistakes. Let's pray.

♥ Line up in front of our constellation boards. I will give each of you another star sticker. As you put your sticker on the board, say a short prayer such as "Thank you for the beautiful stars." *When all the kids have prayed, close together with:* **Amen!** ♥

As they go back to their seats, stick a star on the hand of each child. This star is your reminder that God created everything to be good. He put all those stars in just the right places. And he created us just right, too.

Theme:
God cares for even the smallest sparrow.

Will My Dog Be in Heaven?

Bible Reference:
Genesis 1:24-25 and Matthew 10:29

Simple Supplies:
A Bible and one chenille wire for each child

L ots of Bible stories involve animals. I'll act out an animal, and when you think of a Bible story or verse that involves that animal, join in the action with me. *Pantomime a swimming fish. After several children have joined in, ask:* What's your story? *Have several children respond.*

Let's try another one. *Tip your head down, and "baa" like a sheep.*

Here's the last one. *Flap your wings like a bird.*

The Bible includes lots of stories about animals. One of these is the story of Creation, which is found in Genesis. *Open your Bible to Genesis 1:24-25.* Genesis 1:24-25 says: "Then God said, 'Let the earth be filled with animals, each producing more of its own kind. Let there be tame animals and small crawling animals and wild animals, and let each produce more of its kind.' And it happened. So God made the wild animals, the tame animals, and all the small crawling animals to produce more of their own kind. God saw that this was good."

In the book of Genesis in the Bible, we can read about two times that God cared for animals. One of the important jobs God gave to Adam in the garden of Eden was to care for the animals. Noah cared for all the animals during the great flood and afterward, God promised Noah and every creature that he would never again destroy all living things with a flood. God seems to care about the animals he created. Can you silently act out your favorite animal? *Allow children to pantomime their favorite animals.* We enjoy our pets so much, and we sometimes wonder if there will be animals in heaven with God. What do you think? *Allow children to respond.*

That is a question I can't answer, because I've never been to heaven, and I can't find anything in the Bible that says there will be or won't be animals in heaven. *Open your Bible to Matthew 10:29.* But Matthew 10:29 tells us that not even a little sparrow can die without God knowing.

While we can't know for sure whether there are dogs or cats or guinea pigs or turtles in heaven, we do know that God created and cares for every little creature. He knows what happens to each of them. *Give each child a chenille wire to form into the shape of their favorite pet or a pet they'd like to have.* Hang this little animal up in your room to remind you that God created animals and cares about them.

I'd like you to join me in this prayer. When I pause, you say "for each creature" all together, and we'll all say "Amen" together at the end.

♥ **Lord, we thank you** *(pause)* **for each creature.**
We see your concern *(pause)* **for each creature.**
Help us to show your care *(pause)* **for each creature.**
Amen. ♥

Theme:
The Holy Spirit produces good fruit in us.

How Can People Produce Fruit?

Bible Reference:
Galatians 5:22-23a

Simple Supplies:
A Bible and a small bunch of grapes for each child, stored in a paper bag until you need them

There's a special treat inside this bag for us to share. It's one thing, but it has many parts—enough for us to share. Can you guess what my treat is? *If children have difficulty guessing, give them some clues such as "it is a fruit," "they are green or purple," "they come in small bites," and "they can be dried to make raisins." Then show the grapes to the children.*

You know, I didn't grow these grapes myself, and I didn't cut them off the vine myself either. A farmer somewhere far away carefully planted and tended his plants. He watered them and protected them from bugs and other dangers. Someone picked the grapes and then another person took them to the grocery store so that we'd have them to share today. A whole team of people worked together to bring these grapes to us. In fact, we'll add more people to that team right now. I'll pass the grapes to the person on my right. That person will take some, and then he *(or she)* will pass them to the person on his *(or her)* right. We'll continue around the circle until everyone has some grapes. Don't eat the grapes yet. *Have children pass the grapes.*

In Galatians 5:22-23a we read about fruit that God's Holy Spirit can produce in our lives. Let's look at what that fruit is. *Open your Bible to Galatians, and read aloud Galatians 5:22-23a:* "But the Spirit produces the fruit of love, joy, peace, patience, kindness, goodness, faithfulness, gentleness, self-control."

These things are all good fruit that God can help us have in our lives. How can we produce fruit in our lives? What are some ways we can love others? *Allow the children to share after each question.* How can we show more joy? How can we have more patience? How can we show more goodness?

When someone comes up with the idea of sharing, suggest that children share their grapes with others as they return to their seats.

Let's close in prayer.

♥ **Dear God, help us to bear good fruit for you. Thank you for being with us every day. In Jesus' name, amen.** ♥

Theme:

God is never too busy to listen to us.

Bible Reference:

Jeremiah 29:12

Does God Have a Phone or Answering Machine?

Simple Supplies:

A Bible, a disconnected phone, an answering machine, a tape player, and a blank cassette. Record the cassette using these two messages: a busy signal and an answering-machine message that says: "Sorry I can't take your call right now. Please leave your name and your phone number, and I will return your call as soon as possible."

When something really great happens, what's the first thing you want to do? *Let children respond.* I always want to call my best friend and tell him *(or her)* the great news! *Pick up the phone, and push the buttons.* I just can't wait to tell my friend what just happened to me. I'm so excited. I know my friend is going to love the news. *Tap your foot impatiently.* I think I'll explode if I can't tell my news real soon. *Play the busy signal on the tape player.* Oh no! The line is busy! I can't tell my friend this great news!

Have you ever called someone and gotten a busy signal? How does it feel when that happens to you? *Let children respond.*

Imagine that you're at home in bed, and in the middle of the night, you feel really sick. Your mom or dad takes your temperature, and you have a high fever. He or she is worried and wants to talk to the doctor right away. *Pick up the phone, and hurriedly punch in a number.* The doctor's phone rings. *Stand up and pace back and forth, then sit down and get ready to play the answering-machine message on the tape player.* "Come on, Doctor. Answer your phone," Mom or Dad says. "Finally," he or she sighs. Mom or Dad begins to tell the doctor how sick you are, but . . . *Pick up the answering machine, and play the message on the tape player.*

The doctor's not there. Your mom or dad has to leave a message on the answering machine. How would your mom or dad feel? Have you ever had an emergency at your house and your mom or dad got an answering machine message instead of help? *Let children respond.*

I know someone that I can talk to any time—someone we can call on and never, ever get a busy signal. He doesn't even need an answering machine. He's never too busy to listen. Do you know who that is? *Let children respond.* You're right! It's God! God doesn't need a phone or an answering machine. He hears us whenever we talk to him. God is waiting just to hear from us.

Open your Bible to Jeremiah 29:12. Listen to what God tells us in Jeremiah 29:12. "Then you will call my name. You will come to me and pray to me, and I will listen to you." God hears every prayer. God wants to hear from us. He wants us to tell him when we are worried or sick, happy or sad.

When can we talk to God? *Let children respond.* God loves to hear from us when we're working or playing, alone or with others. It doesn't matter if we're sitting, standing, lying down, or kneeling. It can be in a whisper or talking out loud. We don't have to pick up a telephone or worry about getting a busy signal or an answering machine. All we have to do is talk to God in prayer.

Let's thank God for hearing us whenever we pray. As we hold hands, I will begin our prayer. Each of you can shout out one word of thanks, and then I will close the prayer.

❤ *Pray together, then close with:* **Amen!** ❤

Each time you hear the phone ring this week, let it be a reminder to you that God is just waiting for you to call!

Questions
Kids Ask
About

Jesus

Theme:
God gives each of us talents and abilities.

What Was Jesus' Favorite Hobby?

Bible Reference:
Luke 2:46-47

Simple Supplies:

A Bible; a sports ball, baseball mitt, or anything having to do with sports; a book; a tambourine or any small musical instrument; a watercolor set or anything that represents art; and a large bag to put everything in

What is a hobby? *Let the children respond.*
In my bag, I have different items that represent hobbies. *Pull out a sports ball.* Clap your hands if one of your favorite hobbies has to do with sports. *Pull out a book.* Tap your foot if your favorite hobby has to do with books or computers. *Pull out the tambourine and the watercolor set.* Shout "Hooray!" if your favorite hobby is something musical or artistic. Raise your hand if you have a hobby other than the hobbies I just mentioned. *Ask children who raised their hands about their hobbies.*

Have you ever wondered what Jesus' favorite hobby was? I have. Since his dad here on earth was a carpenter, I've wondered if Jesus liked to work in the wood shop during his free time. Or maybe he liked to read. We can ask Jesus what he liked to do when we get to heaven. Won't that be great? In the meantime, let's think about some verses found in the Bible. We'll discover something about how Jesus liked to spend his time when he was twelve years old. *Open your Bible to Luke 2:46-47.* Listen to this: "After three days they (Jesus' parents) found Jesus sitting in the Temple with the teachers, listening to them and asking them questions. All who heard him were amazed at his understanding and answers."

After hearing these verses, what do you think Jesus liked to do? *Let children respond.* I think that Jesus liked to spend time thinking and learning about God and the Bible. He may have loved playing games and going to the marketplace, but we know he also enjoyed hanging out with the church teachers and talking about God.

One thing I've learned is that we don't have to be in church to learn about God. We can be playing baseball, reading books, painting pictures, or listening to music, and we can still learn about God.

Also, it's important to share with others what we know about God. In what ways can we can share Jesus with others while we do things we enjoy? How can you use your hobby to share Jesus with those around you? *Let children share.*

Isn't it great that God gives us all different talents and hobbies?

❤ Let's thank God for our different hobbies with a popcorn prayer. Any time you want during the prayer, pop up and say "Thank you, God, for baseball (or whatever your hobby is)" as we talk to God. I'll close our prayer after you've each had a chance to pray. *When everyone has had a chance to pray, close by saying* **Amen.** ❤

Theme:
Jesus never sinned.

Bible Reference:
Isaiah 53:9b and 2 Corinthians 5:21

Simple Supplies:
A Bible; a clear glass cookie jar filled with cookies; and three white T-shirts in infant, child, and adult sizes

Did Jesus Get Into Trouble When He Was a Kid?

Do you ever get angry at your brother or sister—maybe angry enough to feel like hitting him or her? Have you ever told a lie or stuck out your tongue at someone? How about disobeying your parents or saying something that hurt somebody? Did you ever take a cookie even though your mom or dad said not to? *Show the cookie jar, and let the kids respond to each of the questions.* Why do we do some of the things we do, even when we know they are wrong?

I wonder if Jesus ever did any of these things when he was a young boy? Do you think he got into trouble? *Open your Bible to Isaiah 53:9b.* Isaiah 53:9b says, "He had done nothing wrong, and he had never lied." Even as a child, Jesus never sinned.

Have three children hold up the T-shirts. We know that Jesus lived and grew. *Point to the T-shirts.* We do wrong things at all ages in our lives, but Jesus never committed sin at any age—child, growing boy, or grown man.

Second Corinthians 5:21 says, "Christ had no sin, but God made him become sin so that in Christ we could become right with God." Even though Jesus never sinned, he came down from heaven to take our sins to the cross. No matter how old we are *(point to the shirts)*, God will forgive our sins if we confess them to him.

Let's pray.

💜 **Dear God, we thank you for sending Jesus to earth to die for our sins. Thank you, also, that he was a great example for us to follow. When other people hurt us or we want to do something wrong, help us. We want to become more like Jesus every day. Amen.** 💜

Nobody took anything out of my cookie jar. I want each of you to have a cookie today to celebrate Jesus' love and forgiveness for us. *Pass out the cookies.*

Theme:
Our attitude should reflect Jesus.

Bible Reference:
Philippians 2:6-8

Could Jesus Do Anything When He Was a Kid?

Simple Supplies:
A Bible, a plastic spoon for each child, and a sticker for each child. You'll need to practice the "trick" beforehand.

I'd like to show you a trick and have you try it. I want to see how many of you can hang a spoon from your nose! *Give one spoon to each child.* Ready? Put the bowl of the spoon on your nose, and let the handle dangle, like this. *Do it yourself, and allow kids a few minutes to try it.*

Was that difficult for you? *Let the kids respond.* When Jesus was a boy, do you think he could dangle a spoon from his nose? How long do you think he could keep it from falling off? *Let the children respond.*

Have any of you ever known someone who was a showoff—someone who seemed to know all the answers and could do everything better than anyone else? *Allow the children to answer.* Do you think Jesus was like this?

Jesus wasn't a showoff! Jesus humbled himself in obedience to God. *Open your Bible to Philippians 2:6-8.* The Bible tells us in Philippians 2:6-8: "Christ himself was like God in everything. But he did not think that being equal with God was something to be used for his own benefit. But he gave up his place with God and made himself nothing. He was born to be a man and became like a servant. And when he was living as a man, he humbled himself and was fully obedient to God, even when that caused his death—death on a cross."

Jesus had the attitude of a servant. He was a servant to God and a servant to others. That means he was obedient to God, and everything he did was something God was proud of. Being a humble servant is not always easy, but it's the best way to show God how much we love him and how thankful we are for all he does for us.

God wants us to be his humble servants, too. Wear these stickers to show that you are proud to obey God! *Give a sticker to each child.* Let's close with a prayer.

💜 **Dear God, help us be obedient to you. Help us reflect the love and caring you show for us every day. Help us to be like Jesus, obedient to you and humble and helpful to others. Amen.** 💜

31

Theme:

Jesus was and is God's beloved Son.

Did Jesus Know He Was God's Son?

Bible Reference:

Matthew 3:17

Simple Supplies:

A Bible; baby pictures of the children in your group, arranged on poster board; and a marker

I love looking at pictures of babies. Aren't these cute? *Make sure everyone can see the poster board.*

What things do your parents do that make you feel like you belong to them? *Allow the children to respond, and record some of their answers on the poster board.* Great answers! Parents love you and take care of you, feed you and clothe you. Parents teach you to know right from wrong and good from bad. Parents teach you about God! Looking at all these beautiful pictures, I'm convinced that all these children have great parents!

How did Jesus know he was God's Son? *Let the children respond.* Jesus was loved and cared for by God. God provided Jesus with earthly parents who fed him, clothed him, and taught him right from wrong, too.

Open your Bible to Matthew 3:17. In Matthew 3 we read about the day Jesus went to the Jordan River where his cousin John was baptizing people. Jesus asked John to baptize him. When John did, the heavens opened up. Verse 17 says, "And a voice from heaven said, 'This is my Son, whom I love, and I am very pleased with him'."

Mary, Jesus' mother, probably told Jesus he was God's Son. Jesus might have known from the moment he was born! We don't really know. But we do know that at the time Jesus was baptized, God made it very clear that Jesus was his beloved Son.

God loved Jesus, and he loves each of us. He has blessed us with parents to care for us. He has given us opportunities to learn good from bad and right from wrong. He sent his Son to live and die for us so that we can have life with him forever!

Let's close with a prayer.

💙 I'll say a line and then you can repeat it after me. Ready? *Pause after each line, and let the kids repeat it.* **Dear God, thank you for being our Father. Thank you for giving us parents who love and care for us,**

too. Thank you for sending us Jesus. I want to be a child of God just like Jesus. Amen.

I have a list of these babies' names. Can you help me figure out which baby belongs with which name? *Have a little fun guessing the names that match the baby pictures.*

Purchase or make a cardboard frame for each child. Write "Child of God" on each frame, and hand the frames out to the kids as a reminder that Jesus is God's Son and each of us is a child of God.

Theme:
God is always with us.

Bible Reference:
Acts 16 and Romans 8:38-39

Simple Supplies:
A Bible and a bag of popped popcorn

Is Jesus With Me Even When I'm Riding on a Roller Coaster?

Enter with the bag of popcorn.
Hi, everybody! It's a great day! Let's pretend we're at a carnival and having fun! Join me and have some popcorn. Would you pass it around? *Take a handful of popcorn, and pass the bag to the kids. Shove the popcorn in your mouth, and keep talking.* Oh my goodness! Look over there; they have one of those radical, rip-roaring, razorback, roller coaster rides! That thing is the highest, fastest, steepest, scariest, most powerful roller coaster ride I've ever seen!

Hold on to your popcorn—we're getting on that ride! Stand up, and climb on the roller coaster with me! *Do the motions with the children.* Sit down, and strap yourself in! Here we go! Up, up, up, up ... *Lean way back as you speak.* We're almost to the top! Are you ready for the big downhill? Hold your hands in the air, and be ready to scream! Here we go! *Scream with the children! Shout these instructions:* lean to the left; now lean to the right; bounce up and down for the bumps—one, two, three! Now hang on tight, here comes the loop! We're going upside-down, so put your head between your legs! Now freeze! *Pause with your head tucked, and let the children quiet down.* Our roller coaster just got stuck! What are we going to do? *Let kids respond.* Go ahead and sit back up.

Has anything scary ever happened to you? Has anything scary ever happened to your family or friends? Do you think God is with us even when scary or awful things happen? *Allow responses to questions.*

In the book of Acts, chapter 16, we learn that the Apostle Paul and his friend Silas had something awful happen to them. The Bible tells us that some men got mad at them, dragged them through town, tore their clothes, beat them, and lied about them. Paul and Silas were thrown in jail, and their feet were pinned down with big blocks of wood.

How would you have felt if you were Paul or Silas? *Let kids respond.* They were in a very uncomfortable position! What would you have done if you were them?

Paul and Silas prayed and sang songs to God as the other prisoners listened. They remembered God was always with them. How do we know God is always with us? *Allow response.*

Open your Bible to Romans 8:38-39. Paul wrote in Romans 8:38-39, "Yes, I am sure that neither death, nor life, nor angels, nor ruling spirits, nothing now, nothing in the future, no powers, nothing above us, nothing below us, nor anything else in the whole world will ever be able to separate us from the love of God that is in Christ Jesus our Lord." Where can we go that God isn't with us? *Let kids respond.* Is God with us when things are scary? Is God with us even on a roller coaster?

Follow my motions while we sing this little song as a prayer to God. *Sing this song to the tune of "Row, Row, Row Your Boat."*

❤ **Thanks for up and happy times.** *(Raise your hands.)*

Thanks for excitement, too. *(Bounce up and down.)*

And when the bumps come, help us pray *(fold hands as in prayer),*

And hold on tight to you! *(Wrap arms around yourself as if holding someone close.)* ❤

Theme:
Jesus was obedient to God in all he did.

Where Did Jesus Go to Work Every Day?

Bible Reference:
Matthew 8:20a

Simple Supplies:

A backpack containing a Bible, a hammer, and a pillow; and a pebble for each child

What kind of car do you think a hard-working carpenter would drive to work? If a world famous singer came to town to play a big concert, where would he stay at night? How do you think he would get from the airport to his concert hall? *Let kids respond to each question.*

Jesus had two jobs that we know of during his life on earth. He was a carpenter like his earthly father. Then, during the last three years of his life, he was a teacher and a speaker. Large crowds came to hear him. Let's find out about Jesus' jobs.

Have three volunteers reach in and each choose one of the items from the backpack. Ask each person to identify the item he or she has chosen. Say the following for each item:

● *Hammer—* Jesus was a carpenter like his father. We don't know for sure where he went to do his carpentry work, but he probably worked in a rough little shed or outside. He didn't get rich from his hard work, and he certainly didn't drive a nice pickup truck. How do you think that Jesus got around? *Allow responses.* He had to walk.

● *Bible—* For the last three years of his life, Jesus was a wandering teacher with a group of twelve close followers. Jesus taught from the Old Testament and added teachings that we can find in the first four books of the New Testament. Of course, his final work on earth was to die and come to life again as our Savior.

● *Pillow—* During the three years that he was a teacher, Jesus wandered from place to place to do his job. *Open your Bible to Matthew 8:20a.* In Matthew 8:20a, Jesus said, "The foxes have holes to live in, and the birds have nests, but the Son of Man has no place to rest his head." We might as well throw away this pillow because Jesus didn't have anyplace to lay his head. *Toss the pillow away.*

After finishing with the three items, continue: When he was young, Jesus went to work in a rough shed or outside as a carpenter. When he was older, he went to work wherever he was. Do you think he got a limousine ride to his speaking engagements? He was willing to live a very hard life to teach people his good news called the Gospel.

How can we be like Jesus? What did Jesus do when his work got hard? What should we do when our work gets hard?

❤ *Pass out the Bible, the hammer, and the pillow to volunteers, and have them each thank God for God's Word, the work God gives us to do, and the nice places we get to sleep. Close with everyone saying together:* **Amen!** ❤

Give each child a little pebble. This pebble is to remind you that Jesus walked to work every day wearing sandals. He would have had to stop often to remove the pebbles that got into his sandals from the dusty, rocky roads he walked on. Keep this pebble as a reminder that Jesus worked hard to spread God's love.

Theme:
Jesus gives riches more valuable than gold.

Was Jesus Rich?

Bible Reference:
2 Corinthians 8:9b

Simple Supplies:
A Bible and a large, clear jar full of pennies (you'll need to know how many pennies are in the jar)

This jar is full of pennies. I want you to guess how many pennies are in the jar. *Let the children guess the number of pennies, and say "higher" or "lower," depending on their guesses. Let kids continue to guess until they guess the exact amount or until most children have had a turn.*

Now imagine with me that all the coins in this jar are pure gold. How much would these coins be worth? Let's pretend that I am the richest person in the world. This jar full of gold coins is just a small portion of all the wealth that I have. One day God asks me to give up all my money and live like a poor person. What should I do? What would you do? *Let the children share their responses.*

Well, this is similar to what Jesus did for us. Jesus' riches and wealth are far beyond what we could ever imagine, but he gave it all up to die on the cross for all the wrong things that we do. *Open your Bible to 2 Corinthians 8:9b.* Second Corinthians 8:9b says, "You know that Christ was rich, but for you he became poor so that by his becoming poor you might become rich."

Jesus became a poor person. He was born in a stable, a place where animals stayed. He spent his first night sleeping in a manger, a feed trough for animals. He didn't have a perfect crib with cushy bumper pads. He had no heat, no toys, and no soft and cuddly baby blankets. How does it make you feel to know that Jesus became so poor because he loved you so much? *Allow some children to share their feelings.* I feel humbled and honored, knowing that Jesus gave up everything for me. And he makes me rich by offering me eternal life with him!

We must be very important to Jesus since he gave up everything for us! This makes me think about what I give up for him. Do I gladly give an offering to God? Am I quick to help those in need? Hmm . . . sometimes those are hard questions to answer.

Let's talk to God and express our thanks to him for giving us Jesus.

♥ **Dear God, thank you for loving us so much that you gave**

us Jesus, who became poor that we might become rich. Help us to never forget that Jesus gave up everything for us. Help us to willingly and cheerfully give to you anything you ask. Amen. ♥

Now I'm going to give each of you two coins. Think of these coins as pure gold. Save one for yourself as a reminder that Jesus became poor for you. Then give one coin to someone else, and tell that person about how Jesus became poor for them so that they could live with him forever.

Theme:
We can talk with Jesus any time.

Bible Reference:
Luke 18:1

When Did Jesus Say His Prayers?

Simple Supplies:

A Bible, a clock with a large face that has hands that can be moved, twelve small envelopes marked with hours (one through twelve), a pencil, scissors, and a copy of the " 'Round-the-Clock Prayer" handout (p. 41)

I magine what it would be like if the only time you were allowed to talk to your family was at mealtime. How would life be different? Would you like living by that rule? What problems might you have? *Let kids respond to questions.*

You know, sometimes my family and I only talk to God at mealtimes or when we go to bed. Jesus showed us a different and better way. He prayed at many different times, and he prayed wherever he was.

I will ask volunteers to come forward, one at a time, and move the hands of this clock to a particular time. I'll give each volunteer an envelope marked for the hour he or she chose, and we'll share the verse inside the envelope. After we read the verse, you can tell me what this verse says about when and where Jesus prayed. *Continue in this manner until all of the verses have been read.*

You can see from the verses we've read that Jesus prayed any time and anywhere. *Open your Bible to Luke 18:1.* The verse for eight o'clock, Luke 18:1, says: "Then Jesus used this story to teach his followers that they should always pray and never lose hope."

Our relationships with our own families wouldn't be good if we spoke to them only at meals. It's the same with our relationship to God. Jesus wants us to talk with him all the time. Let's talk to him right now!

♥ *Have volunteers come forward one at a time. Tell each volunteer to move the clock hands to a different hour and pray,* **"Lord, thank you for listening to me at (time) o'clock!"** *Then say together:* **Amen!** ♥

GO THE EXTRA MILE! Give a toy plastic watch to each child as a reminder to pray at all times.

'Round-the-Clock Prayer

Photocopy this page, cut the verses apart, and put the verses into envelopes marked with the corresponding hours.

"He took the five loaves and the two fish and, looking to heaven, he thanked God for the food" (Matthew 14:19b).

"But Jesus often slipped away to be alone so he could pray" (Luke 5:16).

"Then the people brought their little children to Jesus so he could put his hands on them and pray for them" (Matthew 19:13a).

"But I say to you: Love your enemies. Pray for those who hurt you" (Matthew 5:44).

"When you pray, you should go into your room and close the door and pray to your Father who cannot be seen" (Matthew 6:6a).

"Early the next morning, while it was still dark, Jesus woke and left the house. He went to a lonely place, where he prayed" (Mark 1:35).

"While they were eating, Jesus took some bread and thanked God for it and broke it" (Matthew 26:26a).

"[Jesus] said to them, 'My heart is full of sorrow' . . . Jesus fell to the ground and prayed."(Matthew 26:38-39a).

"Jesus used this story to teach his followers that they should always pray and never lose hope" (Luke 18:1).

"Jesus cried out in a loud voice, 'Eli, Eli, lama sabachthani?' This means, "My God, my God, why have you rejected me?" (Matthew 27:46b).

"Stay awake and pray for strength against temptation" (Matthew 26:41a).

"After he had sent them away, he went by himself up into the hills to pray. It was late, and Jesus was there alone" (Matthew 14:23).

Permission to photocopy this handout from *Quick Children's Sermons: Will My Dog Be in Heaven?* granted for local church use. Copyright © Group Publishing, Inc., P.O. Box 481, Loveland, CO 80539.

Theme:

God gives us the tools we need when trouble comes.

Bible Reference:

Luke 5:15-16

Who Did Jesus Go to When He Needed Help?

Simple Supplies:

A Bible, a can and a can opener, a bottle of juice with a pull-off cap and a bottle opener, a lock and a key, an unsharpened pencil and a pencil sharpener, a paper bag, and one small cup for each child. Place the can, the bottle, the lock, and the unsharpened pencil in the bag, and hide the cups until the end of the message.

Pass the can opener, the bottle opener, the key, and the pencil sharpener to *different children.* We're going to play a short game. I'd like one of you who isn't already holding something to pull something out of this bag. Then find the person who has what you need to be able to use your item. *Ask a child to pull out a single item and find the partner who is holding the tool he or she needs.* Why shouldn't you go to *(name a child who is holding the wrong tool)* to help you use your item? *Allow the child to answer.* Stay with your partner until we finish the game. *Proceed in the same way until all the objects are matched.*

What's the message in this game? *Allow children to respond.*

When you need help, you go to the one who has the right tools. Would you go the person holding the can opener to sharpen a pencil? Or would you go to the person with the bottle opener to open your lock? No! You need to find the person who has just what you need.

During Jesus' lifetime, he did many important things. He needed to *open* God's Word to the people and *sharpen* their minds as he *unlocked* their hearts to God's plan. *Pick up the appropriate item as you say each italicized word.*

Open your Bible to Luke 5:15-16. In Luke 5:15 we learn that "Many people came to hear Jesus and to be healed of their sicknesses." Jesus' reputation grew, and the job got bigger and harder each day. Jesus knew he needed help. And he knew there was only one place to get it. Do you know who had the power to help Jesus? *Let kids respond.*

Luke 5:16 says, "Jesus often slipped away to be alone so he could pray." Every time Jesus had to do something hard or important, he spent time with

God for help and guidance. Jesus knew the source of his power and strength.

We use tools to solve simple problems like opening a can, but some things are a lot harder to fix. We can't use glue to fix a broken heart. We can't stitch up hurt feelings. We can't vacuum up words that we shouldn't have said. Those things take a miracle. We can't do it on our own, but we can follow Jesus' example and go to the one who has what we need—God. He's still the one who has the power to make miracles.

Pick up a bottle of juice and the bottle opener. Seems like we ought to find a tool to help us drink this juice! *Pick up the cups, and give one to each child.*

Let's close in prayer.

♥ *Have the children hold up their cups and pray with you:* "**For pouring out your help to us, we thank you, Lord. Amen.**" ♥

Theme:
*Jesus' pain was
for our gain.*

**Was Jesus Scared
to Die on the Cross?**

Bible Reference:
Matthew 26:39-42 and John 17:1-5

Simple Supplies:
A Bible, a steaming hot baked potato, a kitchen mitt, a plate, and a table knife

et the baked potato on a plate. This is a really hot baked potato! Watch as I carefully cut it open. *Cut open the potato with the table knife.* What comes out? If I took my kitchen mitt, picked up this potato, and placed it in your bare hands, how would it feel? Would you like that? What if I told you really good things would come about for everyone in this room if you would just hold this hot potato? Would you want to do it then? Would it hurt any less? *Let kids respond to all questions.*

If you believed me, you might agree to hold my hot potato. What would you ask me before you let me drop it in your hand? *They might say things such as: "Would you loan me the mitt?" "Do I have to do this?" "Is there any other way?" or "How long do I have to hold it?"* All of those questions tell me you might be afraid of pain while holding a hot potato or of the burn that would be on your hand afterward.

Open your Bible to Matthew 26:39-42. Just before Jesus' time came to die on the cross, he asked God some questions like the ones you just asked. In Matthew 26:39b, Jesus said, "If it is possible, do not give me this cup of suffering" and in Matthew 26:42b, Jesus said, "If it is not possible for this painful thing to be taken from me, and if I must do it, I pray that what you want will be done." The Bible tells us that Jesus prayed in this way three different times.

Jesus believed God's promise—that eternal life would be available for all humankind through his death on the cross—but his questions show his dread or fear of the pain he would experience.

There was no easy out for Jesus—no way for him to protect himself from the pain of the cross. Yet he went willingly because he loved us and he was sure it was what God wanted him to do. In John 17:1-5, we read that Jesus knew that when it was all over, eternal life awaited those who believed, and the glory he had before the world began would be given back to him. His suffering would be for a limited time, but the results would last forever.

I won't ask anyone here to hold this hot potato, but I want you to remember Jesus, who was willing to suffer pain for our eternal life.

Let's pray together.

💜 **Dear God, we thank you that Jesus was brave for us. We're grateful for Jesus' love and courage. Amen.** 💜

Check with a local fast-food restaurant to see if you can get certificates for free french fries. If not, buy a couple of bags of french fries, and keep them warm to give to the kids at the end of the lesson.

Theme:

Jesus has promised to prepare a place for you.

Bible Reference:

John 14:1-3

Simple Supplies:

A Bible, a flashlight, and an eight-inch length of multicolor or gold ribbon for each child

When Jesus Moved to Heaven, Was He Sad That He Had to Leave His Friends?

I magine with me that you are spending day after day with your best friend. Your best friend will be moving soon to a faraway land, but until then, you get to spend every waking moment with him or her. You set up a tent in the backyard and eat your meals under the shade trees. You stay up late and make squiggly designs with your flashlights against the tent walls. *Hold the flashlight under your chin, or use it to make squiggly designs on a wall.* You talk and laugh, sing songs and tell stories. But alas, the time comes to say goodbye. Your friend rides down the street in the family car. The car turns the corner, and you realize you may not see your friend for many years. How does this make you feel? How do you think your best friend would feel? *Let children share.*

Jesus and his friends had to go through a time of saying goodbye also. Jesus knew that he would return to heaven someday, so he talked about it and tried to prepare his friends for that time. *Open your Bible to John 14:1-3.* In John 14:1-3, Jesus told his friends: " 'Don't let your hearts be troubled. Trust in God, and trust in me. There are many rooms in my Father's house; I would not tell you this if it were not true. I am going there to prepare a place for you. After I go and prepare a place for you, I will come back and take you to be with me so that you may be where I am.' "

What a wonderful promise Jesus made to his disciples. A happy reunion was in store for Jesus and his friends. When Jesus ascended into heaven by rising from the earth into the clouds, there must have been some sadness. But Jesus promised to return again and take his friends home with him. The disciples could feel hope and joy, knowing that Jesus keeps his promises.

This incredible promise is true for us today. Those of us who have faith in Jesus can find hope in knowing that Jesus is preparing a place for us in heaven. What would it be like to live in a mansion with God? How do you feel, knowing that Jesus is preparing a place for you to live with him forever? *Let the children share.*

When I think about this promise, it makes me want to praise God for loving me so much. Let's talk to God.

♥ Dear God, what wonderful love you have for us to make a promise like this. Thank you for promising to prepare a place for us and for your promise of Jesus' return. We look forward to the day when we will live with you forever in your marvelous heaven. We love you, God. Amen. ♥

To help you remember this very special promise, I have a ribbon for each of you to mark John 14:1-3 in your Bibles. *Give a ribbon to each child.* When you are feeling down or uncertain about the future, just look up these verses and find comfort in Jesus' promise to you.

Theme:
Jesus will return triumphantly.

Bible Reference:
1 Thessalonians 4:16-17

Will Jesus Come Back to Visit Us?

Simple Supplies:
Postcards received from a friend (or postcards that have been written on), a Bible, and two 10- to 12-inch lengths of mylar ribbon for each child

My really good friend moved away. To keep in touch, we have been exchanging postcards. *Hold up the postcards.* I feel better when I get a card or letter from my friend. Have you ever received a letter or card from someone who lives far away? *Let children respond.*

Someday I hope to visit my friend or have him *(or her)* come back to see me. Until then, we'll write to each other. That way we won't be so lonely.

Another special friend has sent us special letters. Can you guess who it is? *Let children respond.* That's right, it's Jesus. Where are these letters from Jesus found? *Let children share. Hold up your Bible.* Jesus left us lots of messages in the Bible. When we read our Bibles, we keep in touch with Jesus, just like we can keep in touch with our friends by reading letters from them.

When my friend comes back, I plan to have a big party for him. I'll decorate the house and serve treats and play music. What would you do to welcome a friend home? *Allow responses.*

God has a party planned for when Jesus returns. *Open your Bible to 1 Thessalonians 4:16-17.* In 1 Thessalonians 4:16-17, we read: "The Lord himself will come down from heaven with a loud command, with the voice of the archangel, and with the trumpet call of God. And those who have died believing in Christ will rise first. After that, we who are still alive will be gathered up with them in the clouds to meet the Lord in the air. And we will be with the Lord forever." Wow! What an exciting welcome that will be.

Let's celebrate by throwing ribbons in the air. *Give each child two ribbons.* Toss one ribbon in the air and as it falls to the floor, shout, "Welcome home, Jesus!"

Use your other ribbon to mark 1 Thessalonians 4:16-17 in your Bibles so you can read about Jesus' homecoming and what a wonderful day that will be. Let's pray and thank God for the welcome he is planning when Jesus returns.

Allow kids to pray if they feel comfortable doing so. Then close with this prayer:

💜 **Dear God, thank you for sending Jesus to be our forever friend. Thank you that we can look forward to a special celebration when Jesus returns.** 💜

48

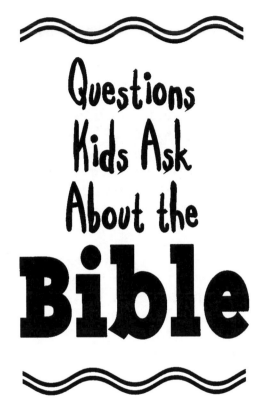

Questions
Kids Ask
About the
Bible

Theme:
The Bible is God's love letter to us!

Bible Reference:
Psalm 119:9

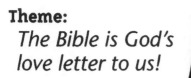

Who Wrote the Bible?

Simple Supplies:
A Bible

I need three children to help me up here. *Line the three children up facing the congregation.* We're going to pass a message from one person to the next. I'll whisper the message into the first person's ear, that person will pass it along to the next person, and so on. It's OK to repeat the message if it's needed because we want to make sure the right message gets passed along. *Your message could be something like "Jesus is the light of the world" or "Who wrote the Bible?"*

Ask the last person to say the message loudly. Hopefully the message remained intact. What a great job you three did in listening and repeating the message. Thank you. You may go back to where you were sitting.

Let me ask you a question. Who was the message from? *Let kids respond.* That's right—the message was from me. But the child at the end of the line was the one to declare the message to all of you.

In the same way, God used different people to declare his message in his book, the Bible. Who are some of the people God used to tell his message? *Have several children name different authors.* Yes, God used many people to tell one message. Some people wrote poetry, such as King David, others wrote history, such as Moses and Matthew, and still others wrote instructions for living, such as Paul and Peter. Even though these people had different styles of writing, they all wrote God's message to us. *Open your Bible to Psalm 119:9.* Psalm 119:9 says, "How can a young person live a pure life? By obeying your word." This means that the Bible is God's message to us about how to live. In this psalm, God lets us know that his Word to us, the Bible, is for us to think about and obey. God wants us to remember his Word to help us live for him. There is no other book like the Bible.

What other books teach you how to live right? What do your schoolbooks teach you? *Let the children respond.* Some books tell us how to eat healthy, and other books talk about how to live a good life, but none of those are God's Word. They don't have the same authority as the Bible.

I like to think of the Bible as God's love letter to me. He loves me and wants me to know everything in the Bible so I can live a life that honors him. When I have questions about life, I can read the Bible, and God gives me answers. When I am troubled with fear or worries, God's word gives me peace.

Let's thank God for his incredible love letter to us.

💜 **Dear God, how marvelous it is that you have given us a message through the Bible. What an incredible gift the Bible is— thank you! Help us to love your Word and to obey it with all our hearts. Amen.** 💜

Theme:
The Bible is full of stories to teach us.

How Many Stories Are in the Bible?

Bible Reference:
2 Timothy 3:17

Simple Supplies:
A bookmark for each child and several boxes of graduated sizes that will fit inside one another. Place a Bible inside the smallest box, place the boxes inside one another, and gift-wrap the largest box.

Who can guess what is in my box? *Let the kids respond.* You can rattle it or lift it if that will help. *After a couple of minutes, continue with the message.* Let's open the box to see what's in there! *Let the kids help as you unwrap the first box and open it and then shake, rattle, and finally open the smaller-sized boxes.* I can't wait to find out what's here! The boxes are getting smaller, but I can still hear and feel something inside. *Finally, open the smallest box to reveal the Bible.*

A book! It's a Bible. What do you think we'll find in here? *Let the children respond.* The Bible is God's Word, a collection of many different stories. In fact, the Bible is like a library! How can that be? How many stories do you think are in the Bible? *Allow responses.*

The Bible is a lot like my big box. When we opened it, we found smaller boxes inside. If we open the Bible, we find lots of smaller books, chapters, and stories inside. *Turn to the table of contents.* This list shows me two different sections of the Bible, the Old Testament and the New Testament, and it shows me that there are sixty-six different books inside. We'll pick the book of Matthew. *Open to the book of Matthew.*

Matthew is filled with stories about Jesus' life. Inside the book of Matthew, there are twenty-eight chapters! Each chapter has at least one special story to tell. *Turn to Matthew 8.* In the eighth chapter of Matthew, I count six different stories!

All of the stories in the Bible come from God. I'm not sure just how many stories are actually in this Bible, but I do know that they are all given to us by God so that we can learn from them. In fact, 2 Timothy 3:17 says, "Using the Scriptures, the person who serves God will be capable, having all that is needed to do every good work." Today when you go home, see how many helpful stories you can find in just one of the books in God's Bible!

Let's close with a song of prayer.

❤ Let's sing "The B-I-B-L-E." When we sing the word "stand," I want all of you to stand up. *Sing this song twice with the children.* Ready?

The B-I-B-L-E,
Yes, that's the book for me.
I stand alone on the Word of God.
The B-I-B-L-E!
Amen. ❤

I have a bookmark for each of you. Put it in your Bible. Each time you read a special story, mark your place, and share the story later with someone you know!

Theme:
With age comes wisdom.

Who Is the Oldest Man in the Bible?

Bible Reference:
Job 12:12

Simple Supplies:
A Bible and a bundle of pretzel sticks for each child

I have a bundle of pretzel sticks for each of you. *Distribute the pretzel sticks as you continue.* Get together with one or two other people, and pretend your pretzel sticks are birthday candles. We are trying to guess the age of the oldest man mentioned in the Bible. See how many birthday candles your group can count in thirty seconds. Ready? Start counting.

How many pretzel-stick candles did you count? *Allow responses. After each answer, ask:* Who do you know who lived to be that old? What age do you consider to be old? *Let the children share their answers.*

Moses lived to be 120 years old. How old is that? What did Moses do that was wise or special? *Let the children respond.* Right! Moses received the Ten Commandments. He led his people out of slavery in Egypt, and he helped them find the Promised Land. It took a great deal of wisdom to know how to do all of that.

Noah lived to be 950 years old! How old is that? What did Noah do? *Let the children answer.* Noah was very wise; he trusted God. Noah built an ark when God told him it was going to rain for forty days and forty nights. The whole earth was covered with water from that rain. Noah was wise to trust God.

As far as we know, Methuselah, who lived to be 969 years old, was the oldest man in the Bible. Now that's old! Methuselah was Noah's grandfather.

The older you get, the more information you take in so that you can make better and wiser decisions. *Open your Bible to Job 12:12.* Job 12:12 tells us, "Older people are wise, and long life brings understanding."

Some people are afraid of getting old, but God says with old age comes wisdom and great experiences. Age is a gift of God!

During our prayer, I'll ask each of you, one at a time, to tell me how old you are so we can celebrate your age today.

💜 **Dear God, thank you for letting us grow older. We need your love and guidance, no matter how old we are. Thank you for letting us be** *(ask kids to call out their ages here.)* **As we get older, help us to become wiser. Amen.** 💜

Take your bundle of pretzel sticks with you today, and remember that with God's help, we will become wiser each year!

Theme:

Scary stories can teach us to trust.

Bible Reference:

Proverbs 3:5-6 and Daniel 1–3

Why Did God Put Scary Stories in the Bible?

Simple Supplies:

A Bible, a watch or stopwatch, a chair or a stepladder for a child to stand on, a raw egg, an empty box, a roll of toilet paper, a bag of cotton balls, and some newspaper to protect the floor under and around the box when the egg is dropped

Have any of you ever been really scared? *Allow children to respond.* Would one of you climb up this ladder and hold this egg for me? *Have the child hold the raw egg out in front of him or her as if he or she is getting ready to drop it.*

Look at this raw egg. What would happen if *(child's name)* dropped it on the hard floor? *Let children respond.* Have you ever felt like an egg about to fall? What can make us feel that way? Being really scared can make us feel a little like this egg—very weak and helpless.

Some stories in the Bible tell us about people who might have had the same feeling. Have you heard of Shadrach, Meshach, and Abednego? They were the three men who were thrown into the blazing furnace for refusing to worship and pray to a statue. Daniel 1–3 tells us the scary story and shares the bravery of these three.

Open your Bible to Daniel 3:16-17. In Daniel 3:16-17, we read: "Shadrach, Meshach, and Abednego answered the king, saying, 'Nebuchadnezzar, we do not need to defend ourselves to you. If you throw us into the blazing furnace, the God we serve is able to save us from the furnace. He will save us from your power, O king.' " But the king was so mad he had them tied up and thrown into the furnace which had been made seven times hotter than usual. Do you think Shadrach, Meshach, and Abednego might have felt a little like this egg? *Let the kids respond.*

I need six helpers. *Choose six volunteers.* You'll have thirty seconds to find a way to keep the egg from breaking when it's dropped. You can use this box, the toilet paper, and this bag of cotton balls. *Hand them the supplies.* The rest of you will need to help them decide how to use the supplies. We want the egg to land safely. *Time the group for about thirty seconds. While kids are working, spread out the newspapers under the chair or stepladder. Have the student who is standing on the chair or stepladder drop the egg and see what happens. You* all worked well together. This egg *(did, didn't)* break. Sometimes our efforts at protection work and sometimes they don't. But Shadrach, Meshach, and Abednego didn't rely on friends or themselves to bring them through that scary time. Who helped them? *Let the kids respond.* And God helps us, too!

Bible stories seem scary at times, but God teaches us that we can trust him in the scariest situations. *Open your Bible to Proverbs 3:5-6.* Proverbs 3:5-6 says: "Trust in the Lord with all your heart, and don't depend on your own understanding. Remember the Lord in all you do, and he will give you success." When we trust God, we allow him to give us strength and courage.

Let's close together in prayer.

❤ **Dear God, at times we get scared — at night, in the dark, when we feel all alone. We thank you for being with us day and night. Help us to remember to call on you all the time. Amen.** ❤

Theme:
God's Word can make your life rich.

Bible Reference:
Psalm 119:72

What Are All the Funny Little Numbers in the Bible?

Simple Supplies:
A jewelry box, a shoe box, a piggy bank, and a Bible

What is something that is really valuable to you? *Let the kids respond.* Most people keep valuable things in special places. *Hold up each item as you mention its name.* Some people use jewelry boxes or shoe boxes or piggy banks. Where do you keep your valuable things? *Allow kids to respond.*

Have you ever hidden something valuable and then couldn't remember where you put it? Some people leave clues to remind them where things are.

Did you know our most valuable treasure is kept in a book? This book is so full of valuable information that you need clues to find all of the information. What book am I talking about? *Let kids respond.* Right—it's the Bible! *Open your Bible to Psalm 119:72.* Psalm 119:72 says, "Your teachings are worth more to me than thousands of pieces of gold and silver." Do you know how to find all of this hidden treasure? *Allow kids to respond.*

Let's take a look at the clues. The Bible is split into two big parts, the Old Testament and the New Testament. *Hold up the Bible, and show the children each part as you name it.* There are sixty-six divisions that we call books of the Bible. What are some of their names? *Help kids as they give names—don't worry about their order.* In each book we find lots and lots of numbers which are really helpful clues. The larger numbers mark the chapters of each book for us. The little numbers indicate each verse.

God's Word is valuable because it can make your life rich with eternal life, peace, love, and wisdom! Let's look for the verse we read today. First we need to find the book of Psalms. Which big section of the Bible is that in? *Have kids help you with each of the clues to find Psalm 119:72.* Yes, I have the Old Testament, and now I have found the Psalms. Next I must find the chapter—119. And last, we need to find verse 72. Great! Would you repeat the verse after me? *Have kids repeat the verse.*

Let's thank God for giving us his Word and sharing his riches.

♥ **Dear God, thank you for the Bible. We will keep your teaching in our hearts, and your special book will keep us in touch with you. Amen.** ♥

Theme:
God's promises of ages past are fulfilled in Jesus.

Bible Reference:
2 Corinthians 1:20a

Simple Supplies:
Two or more Dove Promises chocolates (or other wrapped chocolates) for each child, a Bible, masking tape, scissors, and a marker. Before you give the message, copy and cut apart the "God's Promises" handout (p. 60). Write "Promise 1," "Promise 2," "Promise 3," "Promise 4," and "Promise 5" on five separate pieces of masking tape, and stick one piece of tape on each of the backs of five pieces of chocolate. Do the same with "Yes 1," "Yes 2," "Yes 3," "Yes 4," and "Yes 5," and tape them on five more chocolates.

What's The Difference Between the Old Testament and the New Testament?

Have you ever made promises to other people? What kind of promises have you made? How hard is it to keep every promise you make? What are some reasons you haven't been able to keep all of your promises? Would you make a promise to somebody to do something for them 400 years from now? Why or why not? *Let children respond to all questions.*

The Old Testament part of the Bible, the first thirty-nine books, makes promises about Jesus' coming. The New Testament part of the Bible, written more than 400 years later, tells how Jesus came and made the Old Testament promises come true.

Pass out pieces of candy to all the kids, making sure that the numbered pieces are distributed.

Please don't eat your "promise" yet. I promise you can eat it when we finish. And I promise that it will taste good!

Open your Bible to 2 Corinthians 1:20a. In 2 Corinthians 1:20a, Paul says, "The yes to all of God's promises is in Christ." That means you can read any promise made about Jesus in the Old Testament and be sure that it has come true or will come true when Jesus returns.

Some of you have words and numbers taped on the bottoms of your candies. If you do, please come and get the slip of paper with the same word and number as the one on the bottom of your candy. We'll read the verse that is written on the paper together.

Will the person with Promise 1 read with me that promise from the Old Testament? Now will the person with Yes 1 read with me how Jesus made this promise come true in the New Testament? We'll do the same for the rest of the numbers. *Some kids may need help reading their passages. Proceed with the activity until you've finished all of the numbers.*

The Old Testament makes promises about Jesus. In the New Testament, promises about Jesus come true.

I made a promise that you could eat your candy when we were finished. First let's pray together.

❤ **Thank you, God, for keeping your promises. We learn from your faithfulness that we can trust you in all things, both big and small. Your true promises are our hope for life with you forever. Amen.** ❤

Allow kids to eat their candy, then give them each one more piece of candy to take home. Have them promise to think about God's promises when they eat their candy at home.

God's Promises

Photocopy and cut apart these "Promise" and "Yes" verses.

- **Promise 1**— "I will speak using stories; I will tell secret things from long ago" (Psalm 78:2).

- **Promise 2**— "The Lord himself will give you a sign: The virgin will be pregnant. She will have a son, and she will name him Immanuel" (Isaiah 7:14).

- **Promise 3**— "But you, Bethlehem Ephrathah, though you are too small to be among the army groups from Judah, from you will come one who will rule Israel for me. He comes from very old times, from days long ago" (Micah 5:2).

- **Promise 4**— "But he took our suffering on him and felt our pain for us" (Isaiah 53:4).

- **Promise 5**— "Rejoice greatly, people of Jerusalem! Shout for joy, people of Jerusalem! Your king is coming to you. He does what is right, and he saves. He is gentle and riding on a donkey, on the colt of a donkey" (Zechariah 9:9).

- **Yes 1**— "Jesus used stories to tell all these things to the people; he always used stories to teach them" (Matthew 13:34).

- **Yes 2**— " 'The virgin will be pregnant. She will have a son, and they will name him Immanuel,' which means 'God is with us' " (Matthew 1:23).

- **Yes 3**— "Jesus was born in the town of Bethlehem in Judea during the time when Herod was king. When Jesus was born, some wise men from the east came to Jerusalem" (Matthew 2:1).

- **Yes 4**— "That evening people brought to Jesus many who had demons. Jesus spoke and the demons left them, and he healed all the sick" (Matthew 8:16).

- **Yes 5**— "They brought the donkey and the colt to Jesus and laid their coats on them, and Jesus sat on them" (Matthew 21:7).

Permission to photocopy this handout from *Quick Children's Sermons: Will My Dog Be in Heaven?* granted for local church use. Copyright © Group Publishing, Inc., P.O. Box 481, Loveland, CO 80539.

Theme:
The Word of God is truth for all people.

Bible Reference:
Psalm 75:1, John 3:16, and Hebrews 4:12a

Why Are There So Many "Kinds" of Bibles?

Simple Supplies:
As many different "kinds" of Bibles as you can gather, including Bibles in several different translations, picture Bibles, study Bibles, foreign-language Bibles, and devotional Bibles

Hold up one of the Bibles. Who can describe this book for us? *Let kids respond.* Those are great descriptions—many ways to describe the exact same book! It's the same book, but you each noticed different things. You may know what this book says, or you may never have looked inside. You might have heard good or bad things about it. It is still the same book.

I have a lot of other books here. *Hold up the different kinds of Bibles one by one.* How are these books different? How are they the same? *Let children respond.*

Even though the covers, the sizes, the shapes, and even the words in these books may be different, they all contain the words of God. We call all these books Bibles.

God's message to everyone in the world is that he loves us and sent Jesus to take the punishment for our sins. He shares that message through the words in the Bible, but not everybody speaks the same language. Some people understand their own language better than others. And over the course of many years, languages change.

Because of these problems, God gives us all different "kinds" of Bibles. Some are in English, others are in Spanish. Some have pictures to help us understand what God says to us. Others have study notes for people who want explanations about Bible verses and stories.

The key is that all the different kinds of Bibles give us God's words. They all tell us that God loves us, guides us, and saves us. *Open your Bible to Hebrews 4:12a.* God says in Hebrews 4:12a, "God's word is alive and working."

I'm going to pass out these different kinds of Bibles to volunteers. When you get a Bible, find the verse John 3:16. *Pass out the Bibles, and help kids find the verse.*

Let's read this verse from each of these Bibles. *Have the volunteers take turns reading the verse from each version (help kids when necessary). Let kids respond to the following questions after each reading:* Was that easy to understand? Who might use this Bible?

We've read the same verse from many different kinds of Bibles. Some were hard to understand, and some were easy to understand. Some are good for pastors, some are good for older people, and some are good for people who are studying the Bible. Fortunately, some are good for kids.

The important thing is that the message was the same in every Bible! God loves us so much, he was willing to send his only Son so that we could live forever! God's words are alive and working in our lives, no matter what kind of Bible we are reading from.

Let's pray now using words from the Bible.

❤ *Read aloud Psalm 75:1 as your closing prayer.* ❤

Theme:
God's message will last forever.

Bible Reference:
2 Timothy 3:16 and Psalm 119:89

How Long Did It Take to Write the Bible?

Simple Supplies:
A Bible and a skein of yarn from which you roll a ball of 1000 inches (about eighty-three feet) of yarn.
If you have several children in each age group, pre-cut pieces of yarn that are ½ inch long per each year of age (for example, cut a four-inch piece for a child that is eight years old). If there won't be too many children, bring yarn, a ruler, and scissors to cut pieces of yarn during the message.

How old are you? *Allow several children to answer.* Let's pretend that each year of your life is shown by ½ inch of yarn. That would mean that if you are two, your yarn would be this long. *Show one inch of yarn.* If you are eight, this is how long your yarn would be. *Show a four-inch piece.* I'm a little older than you, so this is how long my piece would be. *Estimate and show a piece demonstrating your age.* A piece for the oldest person in our church would be about this long. *Show that piece of yarn.* A year seems like a very long time to us, but when you show it with a piece of yarn the way we were doing, it doesn't seem long at all!

I thought it would be fun to show you about how long it took for the Bible to be written. *Ask one child to hold the end of the yarn and another child to walk away with the ball. When they are about ten feet apart, have another child take the ball and begin walking while the first two children continue holding the yarn. Continue this process until the ball is completely unwound and your church is surrounded by 1000 inches of yarn. Then have the children gather back together and place the yarn in the center of your meeting space.*

We don't know exactly how long it took for the Bible to be written, but scholars tell us that it was about 2000 years. Judging from our yarn length, that was a very long time compared to our lives, wasn't it? *Open your Bible to 2 Timothy 3:16.* The Bible was written by more than one person, but listen to what the Bible says about itself in 2 Timothy 3:16: "All Scripture is given by God and is useful for teaching, for showing people what is wrong in their lives, for correcting faults, and for teaching how to live right."

God helped writers over the course of those many, many years to write the words we would need to help us live right today, tomorrow, and the next day. The God who made us knew exactly what we would need! The

Bible gives us help whether our lives are this long *(show a short piece of yarn)* or this long *(show thirty-six to forty inches of yarn)*. Give each child a piece of yarn that represents his or her age.

Open your Bible to Psalm 119:89. Psalm 119:89 says, "Lord, your word is everlasting." That is longer than we could show if we gathered all the yarn in the world! God's Word will always be there to guide us. As we close in prayer, I'd like you to pray with me. When I pause, you say "and your Word goes on forever!" Let's practice: "and your Word goes on forever!" Let's pray:

❤ **Lord, your love is everlasting.** *(Kids respond.)*

You gave us your words to teach us. *(Kids respond.)*

You guide us with your words. *(Kids respond.)*

Help us learn to love your word. *(Kids respond.)*

And we all say together, amen. ❤

Theme:
God's Word is food for our souls.

What Good Is Reading the Bible?

Bible Reference:
Matthew 4:4b

Simple Supplies:

Place a carton of milk, a bowl of fruit, a loaf of bread, a jar of peanut butter, a knife, a cutting board, and a Bible on a small table in front of the children. Cut peanut butter sandwiches into fourths, and put them on a serving plate for the end of the message.

Is anybody here hungry? People don't need to be hungry with a whole table full of food in front of them! What could I do with this food? *Give children time to respond. As they mention each item, open the item up and show it to the children. Then begin spreading peanut butter on a piece of bread to make a sandwich.* When we are hungry, we need food to replenish our strength and to keep up our health. We could eat peanut butter sandwiches. This would help with our "hungries" until after church!

How do we feel when we're hungry for God? *Look for responses such as "we don't feel good;" "we're lonely;" "confused;" or "scared."* All the food we need to feel better and to grow inside is in here. *Hold up the Bible.* If we never open it, never read it, and never get our spiritual food, we'll go on feeling empty.

How many times each week do you need to eat to keep your body strong and healthy? What would happen to your bones and your energy if your parents only gave you food every Sunday at noon? *Allow kids to respond.* The same is true of food for your soul. Reading the Bible each day helps us know God better as our friend. The Bible is a guide when we have problems or difficulties. It's a teacher to help us form strong, lasting relationships.

Jesus knew about the importance of God's Word when he was tempted by the devil after spending forty days in the desert without anything to eat. The devil said, "If you're really God, turn these rocks into bread." *Open your Bible to Matthew 4:4b.* In Matthew 4:4b, we read Jesus' answer: "A person does not live by eating only bread, but by everything God says." Jesus let us know that God's words are as important for our spiritual life as food is to our physical life.

These peanut butter sandwiches are to satisfy our physical need right now. Take one, hold onto it, and pass the plate to the person next to you. Remember that just as these sandwiches give us nutrition for our bodies, reading the Bible each day will give us spiritual nutrition.

Let's close in prayer together.

💜 Dear God, we thank you for food for our bodies and food for our souls. Remind us of our need for daily spiritual nourishment from your Word. In Jesus' name, amen. 💜

Print Matthew 4:4b on small cards for the kids to take with them as a "spiritual food" reminder.

Theme:
Telling others about God is our responsibility.

How Can People Learn About God If They Have No Bibles?

Bible Reference:
2 Timothy 4:2

Simple Supplies:
You'll need a Bible, jelly, peanut butter, several plastic knives, crackers, and a plastic sandwich bag for each child

I want to make a peanut butter and jelly cracker. Can you help me? I'll do just what you say as you tell me how to make my peanut butter and jelly cracker. *Follow the kids' instructions exactly. If they say, "Put the peanut butter on the cracker," just set the entire jar on top of the cracker. If they tell you to open the jar and put the jelly on the cracker, turn the jar almost upside down, as if you're trying to dump the jelly out onto the cracker. Make it comical, and illustrate that kids must be clear in their instructions.* Finally, we're finished!

Thank you for helping me make a peanut butter and jelly cracker.

There's something else you can help others learn. How do people know God loves them and sent Jesus to be their Savior? *Let children respond.* They can learn it from the Bible, but let's see what the Bible says about our responsibility. *Open your Bible to 2 Timothy 4:2.* 2 Timothy 4:2 says, "Preach the Good News. Be ready at all times, and tell people what they need to do. Encourage them with great patience and careful teaching." God tells us to be ready to share his love. We need to show others how to follow God.

When we tell others that God loves them and how to follow him, we have to tell them step-by-step, just as you told me how to fix the cracker. Our verse says we have to use great patience and careful teaching. What are some things that you could share about following God? *Let children respond.*

Telling others about God is something we can all do—young or old. Everyone can share the good news about God's love. As we pray today, I would like each of you to think of someone—at school, in your family, or from your neighborhood—that you need to tell about God. Keep that name in your head, and ask God to give you the courage to talk to that person this week.

♥ **Dear God, thank you for loving each of us so very much. I have someone special that I want to talk to about you. I know you love this person. Help me to share just what you want me to share. Help me to be brave and to speak clearly with this person** this week. I know you will give me the words to make your message of love shine through me. Amen. ♥

We figured out how to make a peanut butter and jelly cracker. Would each of you like to make one to eat? *Allow kids to make one or two cracker sandwiches and eat them or put them in the plastic bags to take home.*

Theme:
God's Word is our direction for life, not our salvation.

Bible Reference:
Psalm 119:105

Will I Still Go to Heaven If I Don't Read the Bible?

Simple Supplies:
A Bible, a dark cloth to use as a blindfold, several books, a Bible, and a light bulb

Have the children stand in a line. Create a short obstacle course in front of them by setting the books up vertically. Open your Bible to Psalm 119:105. Psalm 119:105 says, "Your Word is like a lamp for my feet and a light for my path." Imagine you've just begun your life's journey, and you must go around each of these books before your life ends and you get your eternal reward. You have just begun a relationship with God through Jesus. Because of that, you have the light of God's Word on your path. *Have the first couple of kids walk through the course. Stand at the end of the course to greet each child and congratulate him or her on reaching heaven.*

The next person has made a faith commitment to God, but decides that she doesn't really need the Bible, God's Word, in her life. *Place the blindfold on the next person in line, and instruct the person to walk a few steps.* She still fellowships with Christians and goes to church, so we're going to let the next person in line help guide her along. *Assign several pairs to walk through the course together. Welcome them to heaven at the end even if some of the books get knocked over, then reset the course.*

The next person in line learned to love Jesus in a country where no Bibles are available. All he can do is to depend on what others tell him. *Blindfold this child, and have the next person in line tell the "new Christian" where to step to avoid the obstacles.*

Have all the children be seated on the "heaven side." No matter how you got here, you all had one thing in common at the beginning of your journey. Do you remember what it was? *Let kids respond—they had faith in Jesus.* The only thing that matters for people to get to heaven is believing in Jesus. Was it easier for the first person in line to get here or the last? Why was that?

God's Word is a lamp for our feet and a light for our path. It makes the path of life easier to walk. If we decide not to use his Word, avoiding obstacles in life is much more difficult. Everyone who trusts in Jesus will make it to heaven, but with the Bible for instruction, the journey is much easier.

Since we're in a place where we have the Word of God to guide us and friends to pray for and encourage us, let's remember to use God's Word as our light! *Hold up your Bible and the light bulb.*

Today we'll sing our closing prayer. Everyone join me as we sing "This Little Light of Mine." *Have kids sing together as you hold up your Bible and the light bulb.*

💜 **This little light of mine, I'm gonna let it shine.**
This little light of mine, I'm gonna let it shine.
This little light of mine, I'm gonna let it shine;
Let it shine, let it shine, let it shine. *Sing the song through two or three times.*
Amen. 💜

GO THE EXTRA MILE! For a take-home, try to find light-bulb stickers. If you can't find any, get yellow office dots and draw a filament on each one with a black permanent marker. Give each child one sticker as a reminder of God's Word, our light.

Questions
Kids Ask
About
Life

Theme:
God wants us to be kind to others.

Bible Reference:
Matthew 5:39b

Simple Supplies:
A Bible, paper, pencils, and a heart sticker for each child

What's It Mean When I'm Supposed to "Turn the Other Cheek"?

Have you ever had a problem with a kid or kids in your neighborhood or school? Tell me about it. *Allow a few children to share.*

Let me tell you a story about a boy who was having some problems with his schoolmates. Sometimes when Sammy walked home from school, a group of boys would bully him. They would tease him about one thing or another and block his way. How do you think Sammy felt? *Let a few children share.*

Well, one day he went home and talked to his mom and dad about this situation. They decided to look in the Bible to see what Jesus had to say about tough times like this. *Open your Bible to Matthew 5:39b.* Matthew 5:39b says, "If someone slaps you on the right cheek, turn to him the other cheek also." So right then and there, Sammy and his parents prayed for the bullies. They asked God to help Sammy know what to do to "turn the other cheek." In the days that followed, an interesting thing happened. One of the boys had forgotten his lunch, so Sammy shared a part of his lunch, the best part—the chocolate-covered granola bar. Because Sammy showed kindness to the boys, they started to become friends.

Let's think about ways we can show love to difficult people in our lives. Get with a partner. I'm going to give each pair a piece of paper and a pencil. I want you to write or draw one thing you can do to show love to someone who is hurting you. Then we will share our ideas. *Allow each pair to share its idea as time allows.*

What wonderful ideas you have. If you do these things, God will honor your obedience. He will help you through tough situations. I've brought a heart sticker for each of you as a reminder to be kind even to people who hurt you.

Put your hands together to pray, and hold the sticker between your hands.

💜 **Dear God, please help me to be kind to people even when they aren't nice to me. Amen.** 💜

Theme:
We can't earn eternal life.

Bible Reference:
Ephesians 2:8-9

Simple Supplies:
A Bible; three crackers; three balloons that are easy to blow up; and a simple gift for each child, such as a pencil, an eraser, or a balloon. Put the gifts inside three gift bags.

Does God Give Us Grades Like We Get in School?

I need three children to do some things for me. *Line the volunteers up in front of the other kids.* First I'd like each of you to blow up one of these balloons. Very good. Now, can you eat these crackers and whistle at the same time? *Give them each a cracker and have them each whistle if possible.* That's a little more difficult to do, isn't it? I've saved the most difficult thing for last. Can you rub your tummies and pat the tops of your heads at the same time? Good effort, each of you! Let's all give a round of applause for our volunteers.

Hold up one of the gift bags without revealing its contents. Here I have a prize. Who do you think should get this prize? *Allow children to respond.* Well, in this bag I have something special for each of you, but we will see what it is in a little while. *Set the gift bag aside.*

Have you ever wondered if God gives us scores for our behavior? What kind of grades do you think God would give you for kindness to others? How would you feel if you had to have certain scores to enter into heaven? *Allow children time to respond.*

Open your Bible to Ephesians 2:8-9. I want to share a great verse with you: Ephesians 2:8-9. It says: "You have been saved by grace through believing. You did not save yourselves; it was a gift from God. It was not the result of your own efforts, so you cannot brag about it."

Hearing this verse, do you think that God gives us grades so that we can earn our way into heaven? *Let the children respond.* God doesn't give us grades. He doesn't want us to brag about our own efforts. If we believe in Jesus, God gives us the gift of life with him in heaven forever.

You're probably wondering what's inside these gift bags. It's a simple gift. None of us deserves it, just as we don't deserve eternal life with Jesus, but we can receive it freely and gratefully. We can't earn it; we can only accept it and thank the giver for the gift. Our three volunteers get to give a gift to each child here, and they can keep gifts for themselves too.

How does it feel to receive a gift? *Let a few children share.* God wants you to enjoy his free gift of eternal life. Isn't it wonderful that we don't have to earn God's love and acceptance?

Let's thank God for his gift to us.

❤ **Dear God, we thank you for loving us and giving us the gift of life with you forever. Help us to receive your gift of love with open hearts. Amen.** ❤

Theme:

*We are each
special to God.*

Bible Reference:

Matthew 18:10b

Simple Supplies:

A Bible and angel stickers.
Enter wearing a sweatband and a towel
around your neck and holding a jump-rope.

Do Angels Watch Me When I'm Taking a Bath?

Are you ready for some exercise? God gave us wonderful bodies—let's use them! Everybody stand, and we'll do jumping jacks. *Have everyone do jumping jacks.* Now jog in place. *Have everyone jog in place.* Reach for the sky; lean left; lean right; stretch as high as you can; now sit down!

Isn't it wonderful how our bodies work? What wonderful creations we are. What fun things do you do to play or exercise? *Let kids respond.*

The Bible says that God created us in his image. That makes us very, very special to God. What are some ways we take care of our bodies? *Let children respond.* We need to get exercise, get plenty of sleep, eat healthy foods, and make good choices for our lives.

I'd like you all to stand up and look at those around you. Who can tell me how we are all alike? *Let children respond.* Now look around again, and tell me how each of us is different. *Let children respond.*

God made each of us special, and he loves us so much that he is always caring for us and watching over us. God cares for each of us, regardless of our size, shape, color, or age. *Open your Bible to Matthew 18:10b.* In Matthew 18:10b, Jesus says: "Don't think these little children are worth nothing. I tell you that they have angels in heaven who are always with my Father in heaven."

Do you suppose those angels are watching over us right now? What about when we're playing? at home? at school? How about when we're taking a bath? *Let children respond.* God sends his angels to guide us, to protect us, and to help us when we need it. He loves us and wants the very best for us at all times.

Let's close in prayer.

♥ **Heavenly Father, thank you for creating us in your image. Thank you for making each of us special. Help us take good care of the bodies you've given us. And thank you for sending angels to protect us. In Jesus' name, amen.** ♥

I have an angel sticker for each of you to remind you of God's special agents that he sends when we need them. *Give an angel sticker to each child.*

Theme:
God wants us to love others.

Bible Reference:
John 13:34

Simple Supplies:
A Bible, a large red paper heart with the words from John 13:34 printed on it, a brown medicine bottle, and a small red paper heart printed with the same verse for each child. Attach each heart to a piece of string to form a necklace.

Has anyone ever said or done something to you that made you feel sad? hurt? angry? afraid? *Let children respond.* When people hurt our feelings, we have a hard time liking those people. But God commands us to love everyone. *Hold up the large paper heart. Open your Bible to John 13:34.* In the book of John, Jesus says, "I give you a new command: Love each other as I have loved you."

Who is our "neighbor"? *Let children respond.* The word neighbor means all the people we have contact with—at school, at home, in our neighborhoods, or even at the store. How easy is it to show God's love to others? Can you think of times that it might be hard to share God's love? *Let the kids respond.* We may not always like what our neighbors say or do, but we must love them.

It reminds me of taking medicine when I'm sick. *Hold up the medicine bottle.* Sometimes I may not want to swallow hard-to-take medicine, but I know I need it to get better.

It's the same with loving hard-to-get-along-with people. God has commanded us to love them, and I feel better when I obey him. I still may not like what they do or say, but, with God's help, I can show his love to them.

Let's close in prayer together.

❤ **Dear God, we know that in this world others will do and say things that we don't like or things that might even hurt us or our feelings. Help us love them as you have commanded us to do. In Jesus' name, amen.** ❤

Give each child a paper heart necklace. These necklaces will serve as a reminder of God's command to love other people as God loves us.

Theme:
God created everything beautiful.

Bible Reference:
Psalm 19:1

Why Did God Make the Sky Blue and Not Green?

Simple Supplies:
A Bible, a large piece of poster board, a box of crayons, a bouquet of flowers, and a bowl of different-colored fruit. Make sure you have enough pieces of fruit for each child to have one.

What's your favorite color? *Allow kids to respond.* Mine is *(fill in your favorite color).* Where does color come from? *Allow the children to respond.* God sure knows how to make things beautiful!

Select a color from this box of crayons, and help me draw a picture of God's colorful world on this poster board. *Allow the children to decide what to draw. If you have very young children, suggest green grass, fruit trees, flowers, or a sky filled with clouds, a rainbow, or a sun.*

What a beautiful picture! God created the world with some very pretty colors. Think about the blue sky on a bright sunny day or the many colors of a flower bouquet. *Hold up the bouquet.* Why do you think God chose the colors he chose? Why did he make the sky blue and not green, or red, or yellow? *Let the children offer their suggestions.*

Blue for a sunny sky seems just right to us, because that is just how God wanted it. He could have picked any color, and it would look wonderful.

I brought a bowl of fruit. Look at all the different colors in the fruits here! Which ones are your favorites? *Let the kids respond.* God knew what he was doing! He made everything beautiful—the fruits, the flowers, the trees, the oceans, and the sky. *Open your Bible to Psalm 19:1.* Psalm 19:1 says, "The heavens tell the glory of God, and the skies announce what his hands have made." That is some colorful announcement!

Let's close with a pop-up prayer. When you think of something beautiful that God made, pop up and say it. I'll begin.

❤ **Dear God, thank you for the skies of blue. We love:** *let children pop up with their answers.* **We promise to take care of all these things just like you take care of us. Amen.** ❤

I can't hand you a piece of God's blue sky, but you may take a piece of fruit home with you. When you eat it, think about the beauty of all of God's creation!

Theme:
Jesus is the only way to heaven.

Bible Reference:
John 14:6

Are There Shortcuts to Heaven?

Simple Supplies:
A map, a globe, and a Bible

Have you have ever taken a shortcut? *Let children respond.* Some people use shortcuts to make things easier. Others use them to get places faster. When or where have you used a shortcut? Why? *Let kids respond.*

When we're looking for a shortcut, sometimes other people can help. Other times we might need a map. *Hold up the map.* How can a map help? Finding your way can be easier with help! *Pick up the globe.* This globe shows the whole world! Would three of you help me? I've been looking for heaven—see if you can help me find it. *Hand them the map and the globe, and let them search.* Thank you for trying to help me.

We can't seem to find heaven using these tools, but finding heaven isn't hard. God gives us good directions. *Hold up the Bible, and turn to John 14:6.* In John 14:6 Jesus says: "I am the way, and the truth, and the life. The only way to the Father is through me." There is only one way, and there are no shortcuts.

God wants everyone to find heaven, but those who don't know Jesus will never find their way. How can we help? *Let kids respond.* We'll start by praying for people who don't yet know him. Many of you know someone who needs to meet Jesus. As I pray, think of those people. We'll pray that God will help you show them the way.

♥ **Dear God, you have given us one clear, direct, path to heaven. We have no shortcuts, because none will work. Thank you for sending Jesus as the way to heaven. Help us to tell others about you. Amen.** ♥

Theme:
We're created to worship God.

Bible Reference:
Luke 4:8b

Why Do We Worship God?

Simple Supplies:

A Bible and bags of Hershey's Hugs or Kisses. (Stickers or construction paper heart cutouts will work too.)

How do you like getting hugs? Hugs show a special kind of love. Who gives you hugs? *Let kids respond.*
There are all kinds of hugs. There are bear hugs that are tight and powerful; there are group hugs which get very crowded; there are hugs that hang on very long; and there are hugs that are short and sweet. What kind of hugs do you give your mom or dad? *Let kids respond.*

Hugs are important! They show love and care. Would some of you like to help me give a special hug? *Hold up the bag of Hugs or Kisses (or stickers or construction paper heart cutouts), and choose children to help pass them out.* How did this Hug make you feel? *Let children respond.* Giving them made me feel great!

That's the special thing about hugs! When you're giving one, you're getting one at the same time! But how can we share hugs with God? Can we throw him a hug? What about mailing a hug? *Let kids respond.* We can't throw or mail a hug to God; it would be silly to try. So what can we do to show God we love him? *Let kids respond.*

God wants a special kind of love. *Open your Bible to Luke 4:8b.* Luke 4:8b says, "It is written in the Scriptures: 'You must worship the Lord your God and serve only him.'" How can we worship and serve God? *Let kids respond.* Obeying God and honoring him in our lives is worshiping him. And the special thing about worshiping God is getting his love back at the same time! This is just like when we hug someone and they hug us back!

Let's worship God together in prayer. I will start praying, and each time I pause, you say, "we worship you."

♥ **Dear Father, thanks for hugs.** *(We worship you.)*
Thanks for those who give us hugs. *(We worship you.)*
Help us as we pray and read our Bibles. *(We worship you.)*
Hear our songs and shouts of love. *(We worship you.)*
Thank you for your love. *(We worship you.)*
In Jesus name, amen. ♥

Theme:
God's good gifts are all around us.

Bible Reference:
James 1:17

Will God Get Mad If I Don't Finish My Broccoli?

Simple Supplies:
A Bible, a large box, wrapping paper, broccoli, tape,
and scissors. Put a head of broccoli in the large box and gift-wrap it.
Prepare fruits and vegetables for a treat.

I have an incredible gift for the person who can guess what is inside the box. Here are some clues. I'll allow two people to guess after each clue is given:

1. It has iron in it.
2. It comes from California.
3. It may help you live longer.
4. Former President George Bush used to talk about it.
5. It's quite flexible.
6. It's good for your bones.
7. It must keep at temperatures between 50° and 77°.
8. It looks like a little tree.
9. It's made up of clusters of "flower buds" you can eat.
10. It rhymes with "Sarah Lee."

When someone guesses broccoli, let that person open the package. If nobody guesses correctly, choose a couple of volunteers to open the gift. Have them hold the broccoli while you finish the message.

Former President George Bush said he didn't like broccoli. How many of you agree with him? What happens if you don't eat your broccoli? *Allow kids to respond.*

I heard the question, "Does God get mad if I don't finish my broccoli?" Let's consider that. Think of a beautiful, useful gift you'd give to someone you love. You've made the gift as perfect as possible. When the person opens your gift, he says, "Yuck" and sticks it back in the box. How would you feel? Would you want the person to give your gift a chance? *Allow kids to respond.*

Broccoli is a gift from God, just like other vegetables and foods. God won't get mad if you don't finish it, but you might be missing something if you don't.

We only hurt ourselves when we don't accept what God offers or follow his instructions. He's sad when we turn down his gifts, but God is very patient. *Open your Bible to James 1:17.* James 1:17 says, "Every good action and perfect gift is from God. These good gifts come down from the Creator of the sun, moon and stars, who does not change like their shifting shadows."

Let's thank God for all the good gifts of fruits and vegetables he gives us. Let's take turns shouting out thanks for our favorite fruit or vegetable.

💜 **"Thank you, God, for your gift of** *(have kids fill in their favorite fruits or vegetables) !"* 💜

Take some of these good gifts as a snack and a reminder of all of God's good gifts. *Pass out the fruits and vegetables as a treat.*

Theme:
Each of us is a favorite of God.

Bible Reference:
Romans 2:11

Simple Supplies:
A Bible and a bag full of plenty of multi-flavored candy or cereal, such as Gummi Savers or Froot Loops.

Does God Like Me Better Than My Brother?

I have a bag of flavored candy here. Take one piece that is your favorite flavor. *Give everybody a chance to choose their favorite flavors.*

Let's imagine that we threw all of you in a bag and offered God the chance to choose one. Would he pick through the bag saying things like: " I don't like blue-eyed ones," "This one's too skinny," "I don't want that one—he's got dirt behind his ears," or "Now here's a sweet, little specimen with curly red hair and a big smile. I'll take this one" ? *Let children respond.*

Open your Bible to Romans 2:11. In Romans 2:11, Paul writes, "For God judges all people in the same way." I think God would look into the bag of kids, smile, and say, "I love them all!"

Now, you might think you're better looking, better behaved, smarter, or nicer than your brother, but God does not show favoritism. He loves both of you equally.

I'm going to pass the bag of candy around again. If you want a candy, close your eyes, and take the first one you touch as you reach in the bag. You must be willing to eat that candy without any complaining. You don't have to take one. But if you do, you can't show favoritism.

Let the kids choose candy. What was that like? *Let children respond.*

God loves us, even if we aren't the most fantastic kids in the world. This week, be a friend to someone you normally wouldn't pick as a friend. God has already chosen to love that person as much as he loves you!

Let's pray for a specific person that you'll try to be friends with this week. I'll say a prayer. When I pause for a moment, silently fill in the name of the person.

❤ **Dear God, thank you for not choosing favorites. Help me to be friends with** *(pause)* **this week. I know that you love** *(pause)* **as much as you love me. In Jesus' name, amen.** ❤ *Give each child one more candy to take home as a reminder to work on being friends with the person that he or she prayed about.*

Theme:

God wants us to be happy with what we have.

Bible Reference:

Matthew 5:45b and Philippians 4:11b-12a

Why Do Some Kids Have More Toys Than I Do?

Simple Supplies:

A Bible, a flashlight, and a spray bottle filled with water

How many of you think that other kids have more toys than you do? What about better toys than you have? What's one toy that one of your friends has that you really want? *Let children respond.*

I have a feeling that most of us wonder about those kinds of things. I'm an adult, and I have to admit that sometimes I wonder why other people have more "toys" than I do—toys such as houses, cars, TVs or vacations.

There are many reasons why some people have more things than other people. Some people may work harder. Some may be luckier. Others may steal to get more.

One thing I know is that the amount of things you have doesn't depend on whether you are good or bad. *Open your Bible to Matthew 5:45b.* In Matthew 5:45b Jesus said, "He causes the sun to rise on good people and on evil people, and he sends rain to those who do right and to those who do wrong." Let's see what that means.

Pretend that some of you are good and some are evil. If I choose you to play the part of a good person, fold your hands in front of you, like you are praying, and smile. If I choose you to play the part of an evil person, fold your arms in front of you, and frown. *Choose half of the kids for each part randomly, or divide a large group in half.*

The sun is a good thing. This flashlight *(show them the flashlight)* represents the sun. Now stand still while the flashlight "sun" rises and sets. *Shine the flashlight from the floor across every child and back down to the floor.* Did the sun shine on you? Did it matter if you were the evil person or the good person?

Let's think of rain as representing bad things and hard times. Let's have you switch roles for this. If you were playing a good person, now you will play an evil person. If you were playing an evil person, now you will play a good person. *Explain the actions from before if necessary.* This spray bottle represents the rain. We'll have it represent anything that is tough to take, like walking through a rainstorm or not having enough to eat. Stand still while the spray-bottle "rain" falls. *Very lightly, spray all the kids.* Did the rain fall on you? Did it matter if you were evil or good?

The number of toys you have doesn't show how much God or anyone loves you. The key is to be happy with what you have and to accept the best gift of all—Jesus. *Open your Bible to Philippians 4:11b-12a.* Paul puts it well in Philippians 4:11b-12a. He says, "I have learned to be satisfied with the things I have and with everything that happens. I know how to live when I am poor, and I know how to live when I have plenty. I have learned the secret of being happy at any time in everything that happens."

God wants the best for us. God's best for us might be great parents, great teachers, strong muscles, or a great church. His best for us might not mean more toys. God wants us to be happy with what we have. We surely have a lot when we have God's love.

Let's thank God for what he's given us other than toys.

❤ Jump up and call out prayers like: "Thank you God for sending Jesus," "Thank you God for my brother," and "Thank you God for keeping me healthy!" ❤

GO THE EXTRA MILE! Give each child a small piece of paper and a pencil. Paper from note pads in the shape of an animal would be memorable. Have them write one thing they're thankful for other than toys and put it in their pockets to think about during the day.

Theme:
God's love never ends.

Bible Reference:
Psalm 136:1-3, 23-26 and Jeremiah 31:3b

Simple Supplies:
A hula hoop and a Bible

Will God Love Me No Matter What?

Begin by spinning the hula hoop around your waist or on your arm. Would some of you like to try it? *Allow a few of the kids to spin the hula hoop for a couple of minutes.* It goes round and round and round, and it never seems to end. Where does the circle begin? *Let students respond.*

Have one child hold the hula hoop so everyone can see. Take your hand and run it around the hoop. Does the circle end? No, the circle goes on and on.

God says his love goes on and on—a little like our circle! *Open your Bible to Jeremiah 31:3b.* In Jeremiah 31:3b, God tells us, "I love you people with a love that will last forever." How long is forever? Can we count forever? Everyone raise both of your hands, and let's count. *Count all of the kids' hands.* Is that forever? Well, hold up your hands again, and wiggle your fingers. *Count the kids' fingers.* Is that enough for forever? Maybe we should have everyone in the congregation hold up their hands. Is that enough? OK. Everyone in the congregation, please hold up your hands and wiggle your fingers. Is that enough? No, it isn't enough.

Look at our hula hoop again. Remember that it is a circle that goes on and on and on. It never ends. That's just like God's love. God's love will go on and on forever. It has no end!

Let's thank God together for his love. Repeat these words from Psalm 136: "His love continues forever." *Have kids repeat those words once or twice and then say Psalm 136:1-3, 23-26 as a responsive prayer:*

♥ **Teacher: Give thanks to the Lord because he is good.**
Kids: His love continues forever.
Teacher: Give thanks to the God of gods.
Kids: His love continues forever.
Teacher: Give thanks to the Lord of lords.
Kids: His love continues forever.
Teacher: He remembered us when we were in trouble.
Kids: His love continues forever.
Teacher: He freed us from our enemies.

Kids: His love continues forever.

Teacher: He gives food to every living creature.

Kids: His love continues forever.

Teacher: Give thanks to the God of heaven.

Kids: His love continues forever.

Amen. ❤

Isn't that a wonderful thought? God will love us no matter what. He will forgive us if we ask him to. He will listen to us when we talk to him. He will watch over us. And he will love us, with a love and that goes on and on and on forever.

Theme:
God wants us to pray for people who hurt us.

Bible Reference:
Matthew 5:44-45a

Simple Supplies:
A baseball card for each child and a Bible. Have several baseball cards representing several different teams.

Do I Have to Be Nice to the Kid Who Stole My Baseball Card?

Give each child a baseball card. Are any of you serious baseball-card collectors? *Let kids respond.* I've read about people who collect baseball cards throughout their lives. Baseball cards in good condition can be traded or sold years later for much more than their original price. If you are a collector, you always want to keep your cards clean and undamaged.

We're going to play a short game with our baseball cards. The object of the game is to collect as many cards from the same team as you can. When I point to you, you can ask for a card to match the one in your hand. If someone else has a card from that team, they'll need to give it to the person who asked. If you give up your card, you'll have no chance to ask for others when I point to you. *Play the game according to your rules. Soon you will have a couple of kids with lots of cards and a number of kids with none! Collect the cards.*

How did you feel about this game? *Most children will feel that it was unfair; some may even be angry.* It almost seemed as though I was letting some children steal the cards from others. Maybe you've had an experience like this in your own life—having something important taken from you. Do you remember that feeling? What did you want to do? *Allow a couple of children to share their feelings.* Stealing hurts us! Usually when we feel hurt, we don't want to be kind to the one who hurt us.

Jesus knew that. When he was sharing very important life secrets with a group of followers, he talked about situations where people felt hurt. *Open your Bible to Matthew 5:44-45a.* In Matthew 5:44-45a, Jesus said: "But I say to you, love your enemies. Pray for those who hurt you. If you do this, you will be true children of your Father in heaven."

I want each of you to have one of these baseball cards. *Have kids pass the cards back to their original owners.*

Jesus knows that it is hard for us to be kind to someone who has stolen from us, embarrassed us, or hurt us in some other way. We need to ask for his help in praying for our enemies and being kind to them.

Take your card home, and take care of it like a collector would. You may not ever trade it or sell it for a profit, but it can remind you of something far more valuable—to follow Jesus' command to pray for those who hurt you and be kind to them.

Let's close together in prayer.

❤ **Dear God, help us show that we are truly your children by loving those who hurt us. Help us as we pray for them and treat them with kindness. Amen.** ❤

Theme:
We bloom with Jesus living in and through us.

How Can Jesus Live Inside My Heart?

Bible Reference:
John 15:1-2, 4-5

Simple Supplies:

A Bible; a medium- to large-sized plant; scissors or pruning shears; a basket of gardening tools (a trowel, a watering can, seed packets, and empty pots); and gardening clothes (overalls, an apron, a straw hat, gloves, and rubber boots)

As you begin, have some kids put on the gardening clothes. Have another child hold the basket of gardening tools. Do any of you like to garden? We've got some items here that gardeners use. Can you tell me about some of them? *Give children time to respond. Prompt them to mention the tools in the basket and the special clothes.* A gardener's work is very important. What does a gardener do?

Hold up the plant and the pruning shears or scissors. One day Jesus told his friends, "I am the true vine; my Father is the gardener. He cuts off every branch of mine that does not produce fruit. And he trims and cleans every branch that produces fruit so that it will produce even more fruit." If I trim this plant *(snip off one of the branches, leaves, or vines)*, it might look like it hurts the plant. Does it? Pruning helps plants to grow thicker, stronger, and fuller.

Set the plant down, and hold up the part you cut off. If this branch lays here on its own, what will happen to it? *Allow children to respond.* It'll dry up and die. It needs nourishment to stay alive because it is part of the plant. Jesus told his friends, "I am the vine, and you are the branches." We need Jesus to help us grow. *Open your Bible to John 15:4.* In John 15:4, Jesus said, "Remain in me, and I will remain in you. A branch cannot produce fruit alone but must remain in the vine. In the same way, you cannot produce fruit alone but must remain in me."

As we grow in Jesus, he will help us to branch out and touch other people with his love. The fruit we can produce with Jesus as the vine of our life is sharing his love with others around us as we obey him.

Plants and flowers around us can remind us of the life we have because of Jesus. We'll use this plant *(hold up the potted plant)* in our prayer time as we thank God for the many blessings he gives to us. I will start the prayer and then I'll pass the plant to the person on my right. After everyone has said a thank you prayer, I'll close the prayer.

♥ **Dear God, thank you for loving me just as I am.** *Pass the* *plant until it goes around the whole circle, then close the prayer.* **Each of us is special to you, Jesus, and we thank you for that. Amen.** ❤

Bring enough small plants or flower starts that each child can take one home. Place them in small cups or minipots. Use this to remind the kids that Jesus is the vine and we are his branches to touch the world.

Theme:
God gives each of us freedom of choice.

Bible Reference:
John 3:16

Will All My Family and Friends Go to Heaven?

Simple Supplies:

A Bible and two wrapped packages. One of the packages should be wrapped with pretty paper and bows and contain an old stick or stone; the other package should be wrapped with newspaper and contain a bag of candy (with enough candy for each child to have some).

Set out the two packages. We have two packages here. Look at them carefully, then without saying anything, decide which one you would choose if you could. When I count to three, pull your ear if you would pick this one *(point to one of the packages),* and pat your head if this one is your choice. *Point to the second package.* Ready? One, two, three! *Watch for the responses.*

Life is sometimes like these packages. We have to make choices, and they're not always easy. What kinds of choices have you already made today? *Kids may say things like "when to get up," "what to wear," or "what kind of cereal to have."* These are all important choices for today. Some choices are even more lasting—they may last for life. We choose friends, and someday we'll choose where to go to college or what work to do. Then there is the choice for forever—whether or not to believe in Jesus!

Jesus made a choice. He gave up everything to come to earth for you and me. *Open your Bible to John 3:16.* John 3:16 tells us, " 'God loved the world so much that he gave his one and only Son so that whoever believes in him may not be lost, but have eternal life.' " That's such good news! It means that everyone—moms, dads, sisters, brothers, and friends—has a choice. Jesus died for the sins of each of us, but he doesn't force us to believe him. Will our friends choose to believe in Jesus? They have to decide for themselves. You have to decide for yourself too.

We had a funny way to make a choice on these packages. Most of you pulled your ear to choose this fancy wrapped gift. *(Name a child),* will you open it for us? *Have the child hold up what's inside.* What were you expecting? Let's open the other package. *Have another child open this package.* Looks like there's enough for each of us to have a piece of candy.

Pass out the candy. If you would like, you may choose to take a piece of candy when the box comes to you. Jesus' love is sweet and wonderful, and he gives it to us freely! We just have to make the choice to accept what he's done for us.

Let's close in prayer together.

❤ **Thank you, Lord, for sending Jesus to offer us eternal life. We love you, Lord, and we want to follow you. Amen.** ❤

Bible Reference Index

Theme Index